Easy Activities for Using Kid Pix® Software in the Classroom

BY JOAN NOVELLI

SCHOLASTIC
PROFESSIONAL BOOKS

NEW YORK • TORONTO • LONDON • AUCKLAND • SYDNEY
MEXICO CITY • NEW DELHI • HONG KONG

Many thanks to the creative teachers

who generously offered to share their ideas

for this book.

Kid Pix © 2001 The Learning Company. Used with permission.
Kid Pix is a registered trademark of The Learning Company.

"Traffic Light" by Leland B. Jacobs from the October, 1980 issue of "Early Years," Allen Raymond, Inc.; Darien, Ct.; 06820.

* * *

Every effort has been made to locate each owner of the copyrighted material reprinted in this book and to secure the necessary permissions. If there are any questions regarding the use of these materials, the publisher will take appropriate corrective measures to acknowledge ownership in future editions.

Scholastic grants teachers permission to photocopy the reproducible pages from this book for classroom use. No other part of this publication may be reproduced in whole or in part, or stored in a retrieval system, or transmitted in any form or by any means, electronic, mechanical, photocopying, recording, or otherwise, without permission of the publisher. For information regarding permission, write to Scholastic Professional Books, 555 Broadway, New York, NY 10012-3999.

Cover design by Norma Ortiz
Interior design by Kathy Massaro
Interior samples by Jacqueline Clarke

ISBN: 0-590-96565-4
Copyright © 2001 by Joan Novelli
All rights reserved.
Printed in the U.S.A.

Contents

About This Book 4

Language Arts Activities

Stamp That Sound! 12
ABC Stamps 12
A Is for Alphabet Book 13
Make a Match 14
Vowel Say and Stamp 14
Collaborative Easy Readers 15
Caption Stories 16
Seasonal Stationery 17
A Consonant Game 17
ABC Books 18
Beginnings, Middles, and Endings 19
Silly Sentences 19
Hide-and-Seek Alphabet Book 20
My Own Letterhead 21
Poem Builders 21
How-To Books 22
First, Next, Then, Finally 23
Mini Word Walls 23
Silly Sally Story Maker 24
Memory Books 25
Picture the Meaning 26

Math Activities

Six Little Ducks 27
Greater Than, Less Than, Equal To 27
Math Fact Match 28
Roll It! Add It! 28
Math Fact Bingo 29
Stamp That Math! 30
100 Days Poster 30
Arrays for Math! Quilt 31
Dot to Dot 31
Show It With Stamps 32
Roll and Graph 32
Send-Home Calendar 33
Big, Bigger, Biggest! 34
Sorting Stamps 34

Pick a Pattern 35
Creative Counting Books 36
Line Art 37
Fish in a Lake 37
Number Puzzles 38
More Than, Less Than, Equal To 39
Fraction Fun 39

Social Studies Activities

Neighborhood Maps 40
Transportation Sort and Stamp 41
Time Lines Tell Stories 41
Fire Safety Map 42
Our State in a Slide Show 43
What Belongs Here? 44
Plains, Plateaus, Mountains, and More 44
Classroom Map-Makers 45
Stop and Go 46
Sharing School News 47
What's My Capital? 48
Technology at Work 48
The Great Sphinx 49
Slide-Show Biographies 50

Science Activities

Science in a Circle 51
Read About Science 51
Postcards From Space 52
Collaborative Science Books 53
Stamp the Weather 54
Closeup on Insects 55
Life-Cycle Shows 56
Who Lives Here? 57
Seasonal Stories 58
Animals Are Special 59
Paper Plate Penguins 60
Pop-Up Science Riddles 61

Reproducible Pages 62–64

About This Book

My seven-year-old is a big fan of *Kid Pix*®. What does he like best? "It's really creative." (He really said that.) "And I like all the choices." Kid Pix's collection of more than 2,500 RUBBER STAMPS has a lot to do with this program's popularity. The other tools are equally engaging. My son likes the WACKY PENCIL, which lets him write and draw with lines that are thick and thin, plain and patterned. And, of course, there's the FIRECRACKER tool. One click of this explosive eraser and—"Boom!"—his work is history. But a fresh page awaits. (Not to worry; there are tamer eraser tools, too, including some that let you control the eraser.)

More than a creativity tool, Kid Pix has applications in the classroom that extend to every corner of your curriculum. Though Kid Pix is known for its easy-to-use paint, draw, and type tools, the 1998 version of the software—*Kid Pix Studio Deluxe*—features a text-to-speech tool that lets kids make their pictures and stories talk—in more than one language. Children can write and illustrate stories, then listen to them read aloud in English or Spanish, as well as print them out in either language. Kid Pix has many other applications for your language arts program, and just as many for other parts of your curriculum. A sampling of a few of the ways teachers are using Kid Pix in their classrooms follows.

Slide Shows The SLIDESHOW feature lets young children easily create multimedia presentations. For example, they can retell a story in sequence, creating a slide for each event. (See page 23.) Or, they might create a slide show to show what they know in science—for example, using pictures and words to explain changes in metamorphosis. (See page 56.) Used in this way, Kid Pix makes a great assessment tool, too. The slide show option is also a wonderful tool for recording important events of the year, such as field trips. By scanning in photos and having children add captions, you can create informative slide shows for children to revisit and share with families.

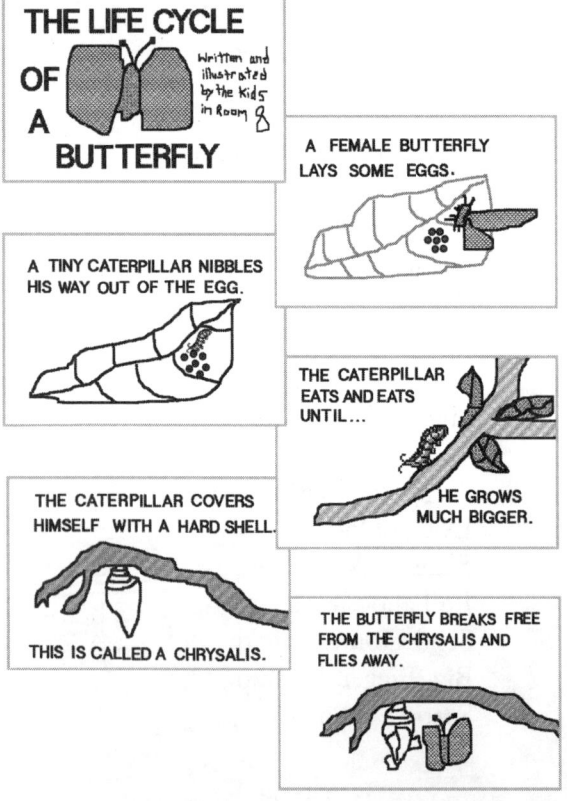

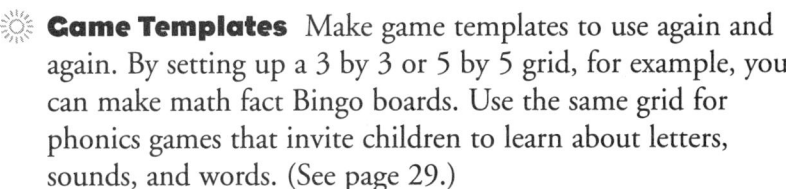

- ☼ **Game Templates** Make game templates to use again and again. By setting up a 3 by 3 or 5 by 5 grid, for example, you can make math fact Bingo boards. Use the same grid for phonics games that invite children to learn about letters, sounds, and words. (See page 29.)

- ☼ **Map Making** Use Kid Pix as a map-making tool. For example, children can make maps of fire escape plans, their school, the community, and more. (See pages 40, 42, and 45.)

- ☼ **Skill-Builders** Make sorting and patterning activities in minutes. Saving templates of each makes it easy to change the activity to support new skills and concepts throughout the year. (See pages 34 and 35.)

- ☼ **Collaborative Books** Create collaborative books based on favorite stories and poems or subjects of study. (See page 15.)

- ☼ **Graphic Organizers** Make Venn diagrams and other graphic organizers that children can complete with words or stamps related to any area of study. (See page 51.)

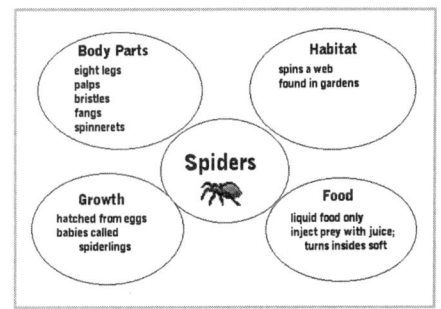

- ☼ **Class Calendars** Let students collaborate to make calendars, creating seasonal pictures for each month and adding notes about school events, holidays, and so on. (See page 33.)

- ☼ **Memory Keepers** Save school memories in Kid Pix slide shows, complete with pictures and captions. Children can create individual memory books or collaborate on a class book. Either way, the process is simple enough for even young children to accomplish on their own. (See page 25.)

You'll find easy-to-follow steps for these teacher-tested Kid Pix activities and more in the pages that follow. Many of these ideas come from creative teachers across the country. If you're new to Kid Pix, you'll find an overview of the basic tools on pages 6–10. From using rubber stamps to creating slide shows with text, pictures, sound, and transitions, you'll get a feel for this program's versatility and ease of use. Kid Pix is designed for ages three to twelve, but is just as easy for adults to use as it is for children. With just a little experimentation, and the right tools, you'll be able to complete any of the activities in this book. Like pencils and paper, Kid Pix will become a staple in your classroom—something you and your students will reach for again and again.

Which Kid Pix?

The activities in this book come from teachers using various versions of Kid Pix, including *Kid Pix*, *Kid Pix 2*, *Kid Pix Studio*, and *Kid Pix Studio Deluxe*. You'll find the same basic features in each, and most of the activities described in this book will work with any of the versions available. What may differ is, for example, the number of rubber stamps available, or special features such as the text-to-speech tool added to *Kid Pix Studio Deluxe*.

Getting Started With Kid Pix

When you start up Kid Pix, the program will open to a blank page. On the left side, you'll see a tool bar. Click on any tool to activate it. Use the options that appear along the bottom to make additional selections—for example, to choose the size or pattern of a pencil point, paintbrush options, and rubber stamps.

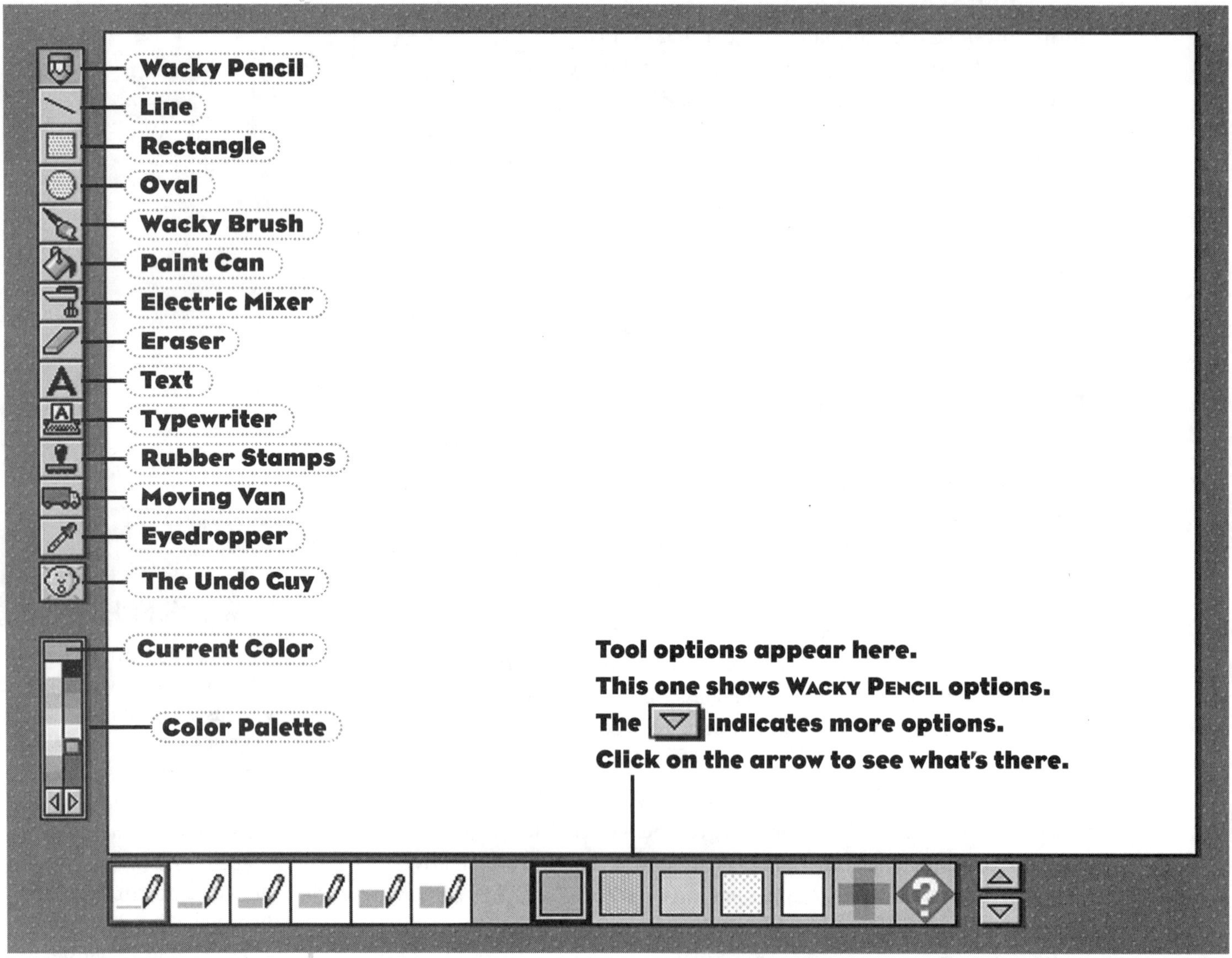

Introduction

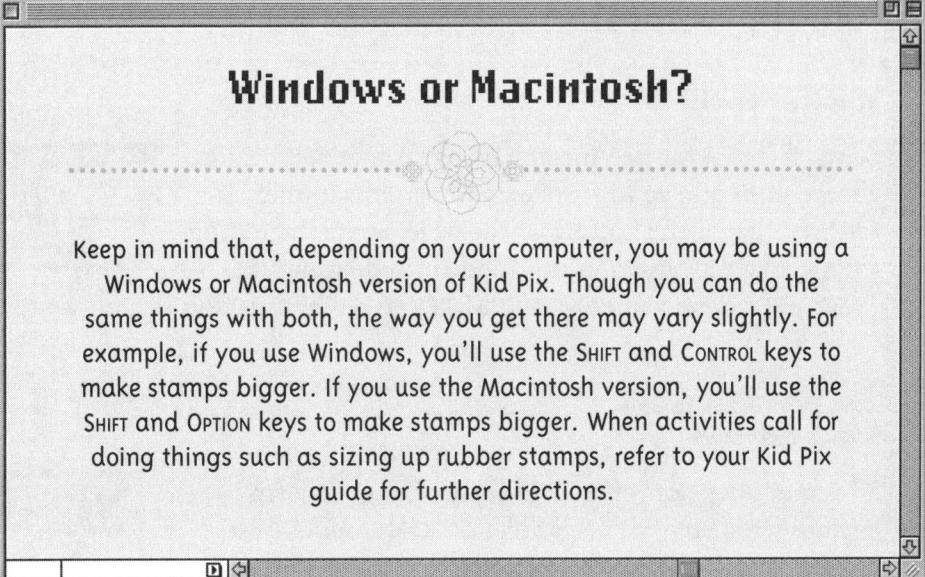

Now that you've opened a page, here's how you can use the Kid Pix tools called for in this book to do just about anything! For more information on these and other tools and options, consult your Kid Pix guide.

To Add Text

Stamp Text

This tool lets children stamp letters, numbers, and symbols anywhere on a page. When they select a letter, a voice speaks that letter's name. (You choose English or Spanish in the SWITCHEROO menu.) To edit text in this mode, use the UNDO GUY (to erase the last letter, number, or symbol stamped) or an eraser. (For more information, see page 9.)

Type Text

To enter text with the keyboard, go to TYPE TEXT in the GOODIES menu. Choose a color and font from the OPTIONS bar, then place the pointer where you want to begin the text. Type as you would with a word processor.

Tip

Sounds or Silence?

Kid Pix tools make assorted sound effects. For example, when you use letters in the TEXT tool (select the letter A in the tool bar), a voice speaks the letters' names. You'll also hear erasers explode, paint pour, and more. If you prefer quiet in your computer corner, just choose TOOL SOUNDS from the GOODIES menu. (That's all—you don't have to do anything with it.) To turn on the sounds again, do the same thing.

Introduction

Tip

More Stamp Fun

To repeat a stamp on a page, just hold the button on the mouse and move the stamp across the page. Students might like to do this to create borders on a page of writing. *Kid Pix Studio* introduced animated stamps, complete with backgrounds, soundtracks, actors, and action options. To share students' animated projects at home, use the SAVE AS STANDALONE option. (Save files to a floppy disk or send via e-mail.)

To Create Pictures

Wacky Pencil

Select this tool for free-form drawing. Before you begin, choose from line widths, styles, and patterns in the OPTIONS bar at the bottom of the page. Some interesting things children can do in this mode include using the WALLPAPER option in ELECTRIC MIXER to repeat a section of a drawing.

Wacky Brush

This tool offers lots of options for painting. You can explore symmetry with the KALEIDOSCOPE option, which creates a mirror-image as you paint. Or, use the PICTURE BRUSH to paint with shapes. For more options, experiment with holding down the OPTION, CONTROL, SHIFT, or COMMAND key with any of the WACKY BRUSH options. Some of the WACKY BRUSHES will change.

Rubber Stamps

Depending on which version of Kid Pix you're using, you may have eight or more sets of rubber stamps to play with. Click on the arrow at the end of the OPTIONS bar to see all of the choices within one set. To select a new set, go to PICK A STAMP SET in the GOODIES menu. Sizing up stamps is easy. Holding down the OPTION key while stamping a picture on a page will double it. Pressing the SHIFT key will triple the size. Pressing OPTION and SHIFT will make the stamps even bigger. (These directions are for use with Macintosh versions. For Windows, do the same thing with the SHIFT and CONTROL keys.)

Introduction

Erase Text or Pictures

Undo Guy

Oops! Change your mind? Make a mistake? The UNDO GUY, located on the tool bar, lets you erase the last action. Just click on the UNDO GUY picture and it's done.

Erasers

An assortment of erasers, accessed by clicking on the ERASER icon in the tool bar, lets you erase all or part of a picture. You can select the size eraser that is right for the job (from little to big), also the kind of eraser. The FIRECRACKER option gets the job done with one noisy blast. FADE AWAY takes a gentler approach—pictures disappear gradually. There are lots of other options children will find interesting, too.

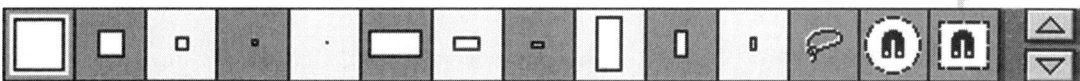

Moving Van

This option, used to move a section of a drawing from one place to another, will also let you delete sections. Just click on the MOVING VAN tool, use the magnet to capture the section you want to cut, then use the CUT command in the EDIT menu.

Move Text or Pictures

Start up the MOVING VAN to move sections of a drawing from one place to another. Choose the right size van for the job, place the van over the section you want to move, then hold down the mouse button to make the move. Let up on the mouse button when the section has been relocated. Another MOVING VAN option is the magnet. This lets you move any size section you want, including a photo you import into Kid Pix. After selecting the magnet, move the pointer that appears to the top left corner of the section you want to move. Hold the mouse button down, and move the mouse to capture the section you want to move. Let up on the mouse button, then hold it down again and move it to move the section.

Introduction

Printing Without Sound Messages

If you are printing pages for which you've recorded sound, but don't want the PLAY icon to appear, you have the option of saving without the sound message in SAVE.

Record Sound

If your computer can record sound, you can use the RECORD SOUND option to add music, special effects, or voice to work created in Kid Pix. Children can record themselves reading stories they write, record captions to go with drawings, or record sound effects or words to go with slide shows. To record sound, select RECORD in the GOODIES menu. Click RECORD in the dialogue box that appears on the screen and speak into the microphone. To play back the recording, click PLAY in the dialogue box. If it's a wrap, click SAVE. To rerecord, click RECORD again. A PLAY SOUND icon will appear on pages for which sound is recorded. To play the sound, select PLAY from the GOODIES menu.

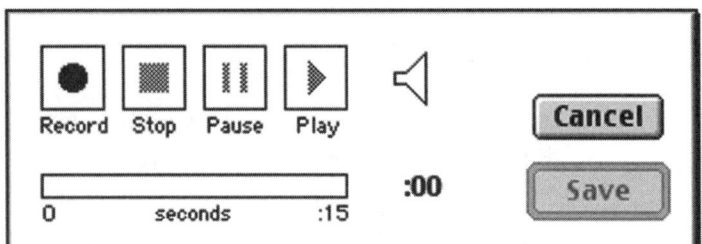

Make a Slide Show

SLIDESHOW may be one of the most versatile Kid Pix features for the classroom. Imagine your students creating slide shows to demonstrate steps for solving a math problem. How about a slide show that shows sequence of events in a story? Or a slide show that lets children demonstrate learning in a science unit on the human body? Observations, including drawings, from science investigations make great slide shows, too. This feature operates like a regular slide show, showing one frame after another, complete with fancy transitions. To create a SLIDESHOW, follow the basic steps on the Kid Pix SlideShow Quick Tips reproducible. (See page 11.) You can copy this page and post near the computer for easy reference. You may want to enlarge the page to make it easier for students to read.

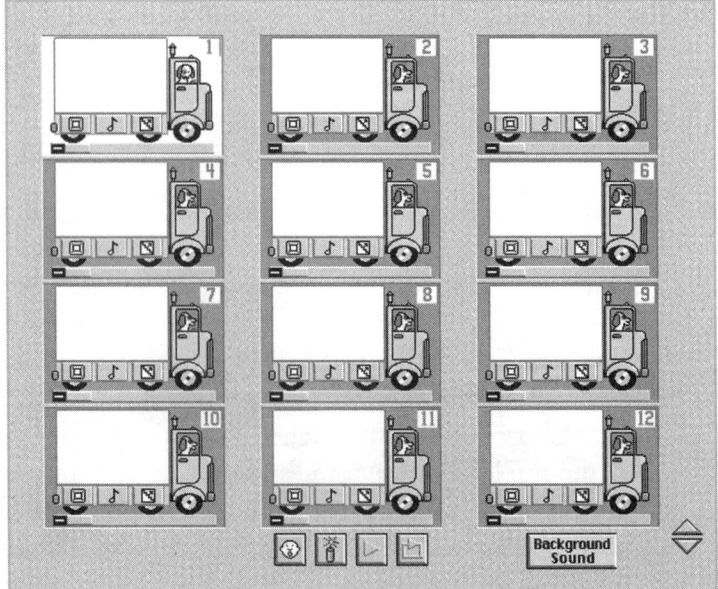

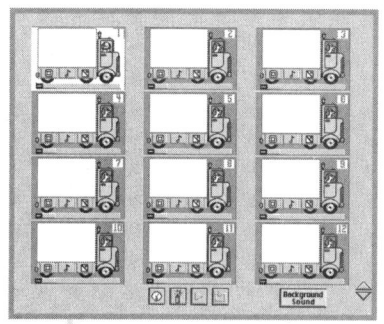

① Open Kid Pix and choose **SlideShow**. A set of moving vans will appear on the screen. The number of vans you see will depend on the size of your monitor. (Use the **Down** arrow to access up to 99 slides.)

② Click on a van to make a slide. Click on the Picture icon to select a drawing. This can be a drawing created in Kid Pix, a drawing from **DrawMe** and **ColorMe** options, or artwork (including photos) imported to Kid Pix.

③ Add music. Click on the , or use your computer's microphone to add your own sound.

④ Choose a transition between each slide. Click on for choices.

⑤ Set the time (from 0 to 30 seconds) that will elapse between slides. Click on the

Time Slide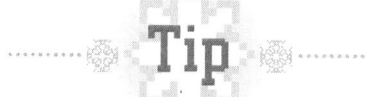

at the bottom of each moving van. Hold down the mouse button, and drag the slider left or right.

⑥ Repeat steps 1–5 to create more slides.

⑦ Preview the slide show. To go from slide to slide at your own pace, hold down the **Option** key and click **Play**. Click the mouse to move from one slide to the next. Make adjustments—clean up the slide show by adjusting the length of time between slides, rearrange slides, and so on.

⑧ Go to **Save As** in the **Edit** menu to save the slide show.

Tip

SlideShow Extras

You can add non–Kid Pix art to a slide show, including photographs. Go to OPEN in the FILE menu. Select the picture you want to copy to Kid Pix. Choose COPY in the EDIT menu. Add these pictures to the slide show in the usual way by selecting the PICTURE icon. To make a slide using a QuickTime movie, click on the van, then go to QUICKPIX. Click on the movie you want and click on SELECT to place it in the moving van.

Send-Home Slide Shows

To save slide shows in a format that children can share with families independently of Kid Pix, choose STANDALONE in the SAVE AS option. Slide shows saved in this format can be played on compatible machines, without loading Kid Pix.

Easy Activities for Using Kid Pix® Software in the Classroom   Scholastic Professional Books

Language Arts

Stamp That Sound!

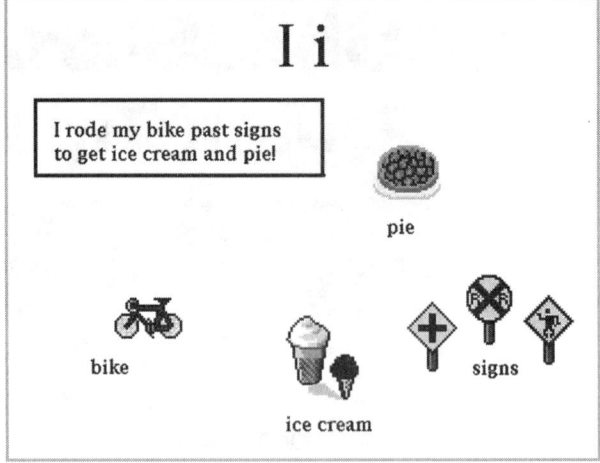

Part of helping young children become lifelong readers is giving them successful experiences with letters and sounds. Kid Pix lets you reinforce phonics skills with fun, easy-to-make activities that will enliven learning. This one reinforces vowel sounds with rubber stamps.

- Open a new Kid Pix page. Use the TEXT tool or TYPE TEXT option to write the letter of focus at the top of the page.
- Have students use the RUBBER STAMP tool to place pictures on the page that contain that sound. For example, for the long /i/ sound in the picture here, one student found stamps for *ice cream*, *pie*, *bike*, and *signs*.
- To go further, students can make up silly sentences with the words for the objects they stamped. They can type these themselves, or dictate them, then type from the sentence you write on paper.
- If your computer has recording capability, let students record themselves saying the words for the objects they stamp and reading their sentences.

Barb Ftacek
Washington Elementary
Mundelein, Illinois

Tip

Make Mini-Books

Children can print out their alphabet letters and stamp squares, carefully cut them apart, and staple them to make tiny books.

ABC Stamps

This activity builds a range of early literacy skills, including letter recognition (upper-and lowercase) and sound-letter relationships. Children can revisit it as often as they like, with a different result each time.

- Set up a table of squares—six across and five down. Use the ALPHABET STAMPS to stamp a letter in each square. Save the table as a template called *ABC*.
- Have children open the template and stamp their name at the bottom. Have them choose PICK A STAMP SET from the GOODIES menu, then choose the RUBBER STAMP tool. From here, children can look for pictures to represent the beginning sound for each letter—for example, *ant* for *A* and *bandage* for *B*.
- Have children exit the program without saving. (The template will be ready for the next child to use.)

Jeraldine Quesinberry
Dobson Elementary School
Dobson, North Carolina

Language Arts

A Is for Alphabet Book

While introducing letters of the alphabet and the sounds they make, start up a Kid Pix SLIDESHOW to let children learn more.

- Review with children how to create a slide in SLIDESHOW. You might even print a blank MOVING VAN, enlarge it, then label the tools children will use. (See page 10.)

- Introduce a letter. Ask children to look around the room for objects that start with that letter. Explain to children that they are going to look for rubber stamps in Kid Pix that start with that letter. They can also use the WACKY PENCIL or BRUSH to create their own pictures for that letter.

- Have a volunteer use the WACKY PENCIL to draw the letter on the blank page. Then let children take turns adding and labeling pictures for that letter. Have children use the RECORD SOUND option in the GOODIES menu to add sound messages to each page. (Children can record the letter and words on the page.)

- Use the SLIDESHOW feature to place each page in a slide show. Print out pages to make a class book. As students learn new letters and create new pages, add on to both the slide show and the book. (Bind the book with O-rings to make it easy to insert new pages.) Encourage students to revisit the slide show and book often, reading the letters, words, and sentences.

- Store completed Kid Pix slide show pages in a clearly labeled folder on a disk or hard drive.

Barbara Cambron and Pam Levitch
Eliahu Academy
Louisville, Kentucky

Tip

Enlarging Stamps and Labeling Pictures

This is a good time to show children how to enlarge rubber stamps so that they show up better on the slides. (See page 8.) To assist young children in labeling their pictures, let them dictate the words for their objects. Write their words on paper, then let them type them on the screen.

Best Bets for Background Colors

Children can go to the GOODIES menu to select background colors for their slides in solids or patterns. Solid colors typically result in crisper slide shows. However, students really enjoy the patterns. Try to guide children in making choices that result in the best quality slides.

Language Arts

Tip

Make More Games

You can use the same format to make other kinds of matching games. For example, make cards that pair books and characters, upper- and lowercase letters, word endings, or words and pictures. Brainstorm more ideas with your students. These games will be easy for students to make themselves!

Make a Match

Make matching games that reinforce letter and word recognition. For example, if you're focusing on vowel sounds, use Kid Pix to make sets of cards that show objects/words that share a vowel sound (for example, *cat/bat*; *pet/bed*; *fish/pig*). Students can use the cards to play a matching game, turning all of the cards face down, then taking turns flipping over two cards at a time to try to make a match. To make the cards:

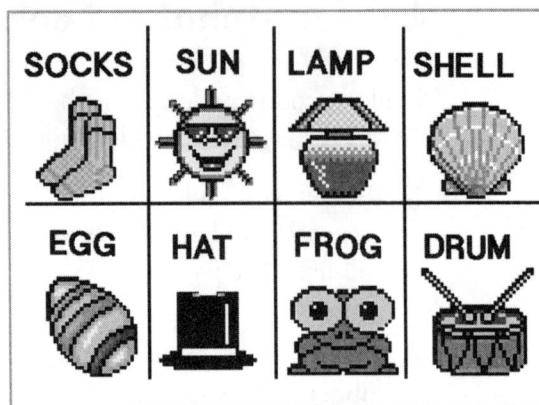

- Open a new page and use the LINE tool to divide it into an even number of cards. (Eight works well.)
- Use the TYPE TEXT option to write a word on each card. Use the RUBBER STAMP tool to add a picture to go with each word. Make sure each card has a match.
- When you've filled one page, save it. Then open a new page to continue creating cards for your matching game.
- Print each page and cut apart the cards. (You may wish to laminate the pages first.) Store cards in reclosable sandwich bags.

Vowel Say and Stamp

This easy-to-make game will build students' recognition of letters and sounds, giving them tools they need to blend sounds and form words. To set up the game, make a template, using the LINE tool to divide the page into 12 squares (a 3 by 4 grid). Use the TEXT tool to label the page according to the vowel sound you're teaching; let's say, /a/ as in *cat*. Use the RUBBER STAMP tool to place a picture that represents that sound in one box. Type the word for that picture. Have children complete the boxes by stamping additional pictures that represent that vowel sound. Those who are able can type the word as well.

Variation: Follow the same steps to make templates for reinforcing phonograms, initial consonant sounds, and other phonics skills. Just type the skill at the top of the page, stamp a sample, and let children continue.

Collaborative Easy Readers

Many teachers use repetitive books to give young children success with early reading experiences. *Ray's Readers* (Sage Publications) are popular repetitive books, with one for each letter of the alphabet. You can use Kid Pix to take these little books further, making more books with repetitive text to share. The idea that follows, based on *The Cat Called* (book 3 in the series), gives children a chance to learn one another's names, too. Adapt it for other books in this and similar series.

- Share *The Cat Called* with students. This story repeats "The cat called…" on each page: "The cat called the crab. The cat called the cricket. The cat called the clown…"

- Set up a Kid Pix template for children to use, typing the words "The cat called _____." Leave a blank for children to fill in their name.

- Have children take turns completing the page, using the TEXT tool or TYPE TEXT option to add their name, and the stamps and drawing tools to make their own picture of a cat.

- Print pages and bind to make a class easy reader. Let children take the book home and share their reading success with their family.

Judy Oleson
Deuel Elementary School
Cedar Lake, South Dakota

Language Arts

Caption Stories

COLORME (in the GOODIES menu) is a collection of Kid Pix pictures that will inspire a range of writing activities. When children click on the picture they want, it will appear on the screen. From here, they can use the WACKY BRUSH tool to color in the picture. Have children go further by using the TYPE TEXT option to add captions that tell about their pictures. Suggestions for variations on this activity follow.

- Let children make "I Spy" riddles to go with the pictures.
- Focus on descriptive writing. Ask children to list as many words as they can to describe the picture.
- Explore alliteration. After introducing this literary element with a tongue twister, have children use the TYPE TEXT option to write alliterative sentences to go with their pictures.

You might assign children to a particular picture and writing activity, then have them each print a page to make a class book. Or, children can write captions for several COLORME pictures of their choosing and print out their pages to make individual books.

Lynn Foust
Emily Dickinson School
Bozeman, Montana

Language Arts

Seasonal Stationery

Create a set of class stationery to use for special occasions or any day. It's so easy that your students will take over to make more. Start with a blank page. Use the RUBBER STAMP tool to make a border on the page. Choose stamps that signify a seasonal or holiday theme. Hold down the mouse to repeat stamps on the page if desired. Let students use the paper to write seasonal stories and/or letters. Suggestions include:

- Write a story each month about something memorable that happens at school or home.
- Write a letter to someone special each month. (For example, in November a student might use the stationery to write to a family member, telling why they're thankful for this person.)
- Use the stationery for keeping a yearlong science log. Make stationery for each month and put pages together to make blank books. Have students record observations about seasonal changes.

A Consonant Game

Set up a consonant game students can play again and again to reinforce letter-sound correspondence and develop tools for blending sounds and forming words. Make a game template by using the LINE tool to divide the page into eight sections. (Draw three horizontal lines and one vertical line across the middle.) Use the TEXT tool to stamp one consonant in each box. Then let children use the RUBBER STAMP tool to stamp objects that start with the designated letter in each box. You can make new game boards focusing on different consonants for children to complete, as well as let your students use the template to make consonant games of their own.

Variation: Play the game in reverse, stamping pictures that start with the same consonant in each box and letting children stamp the corresponding letters. Use the same format to reinforce initial consonant digraphs, such as *sh*, *ch*, *th*, and *wh*.

Charlotte Sassman and Regina Woods
Alice Carlson Applied Learning Center
Fort Worth, Texas

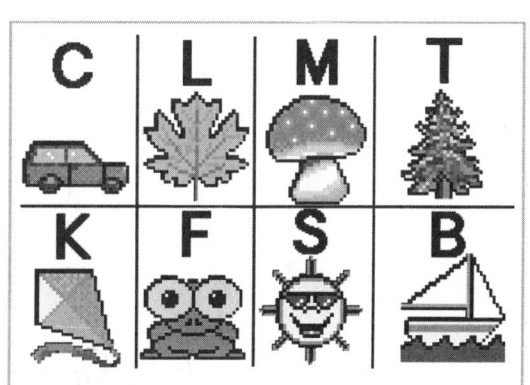

Tip

A Pocketful of Stories

Cut pocket folders in two at the center to make two separate pockets. Give one to each child. Have children write their name on the pockets and decorate them. Tack up pockets to a bulletin board or wall and let children store their seasonal stories inside, one behind the other. Throughout the year, invite children to read the board, taking time to appreciate one another's seasonal stories. At the end of the year, have each child put the pages together in order and add front and back covers. Your students will have a year of stories to share with their families—and memories to treasure long after the year is over.

Adapted from *Interactive Bulletin Boards: September to June* (Scholastic Professional Books, 1998). Other titles in the series include *Interactive Bulletin Boards: Math* and *Interactive Bulletin Boards: Language Arts*.

Language Arts

Tip

Letter of the Week

If you use the "letter-of-the-week" approach, or if you are focusing on a particular letter for another reason (for example, to help young children make connections between the first letter of their name and other words), let students use Kid Pix to make mini-books that reinforce that letter. Children can create covers for the letter, then use additional pages to stamp or draw pictures that start with that letter, and write (or record) words for those pictures.

ABC Books

Alphabet books make wonderful models for children's own books. They generally have an easy-to-follow format, and easily inspire add-ons. As you use alphabet books to introduce letters and sounds (and just for fun), give children a chance to make their own.

- Collect an assortment of alphabet books to share with students. Discuss what students like best about each—the pictures, words, colors, layout, and so on.
- Divide the class into groups. Each group will produce an alphabet book.
- Have each group choose an alphabet book as a model (or let children come up with their very own ideas if they wish). For example, children might like to make alphabet books modeled after Lois Ehlert's *Eating the Alphabet* (Harcourt Brace, 1989), illustrating a fruit or vegetable for each letter of the alphabet.
- Have children in each group work together to create the book, using the Kid Pix tools to create text and pictures.
- Print out pages for each book and bind. You can also copy pages into the SLIDESHOW feature for an interactive alphabet book that combines text, pictures, and sound.

Variation: Have children create alphabet books to support any topic of study—for example, culminate an ocean unit by having each child choose a letter, then name and illustrate an ocean animal for that letter and include a fact.

Martine Wayman
Kenmore Elementary School
Kenmore, Washington

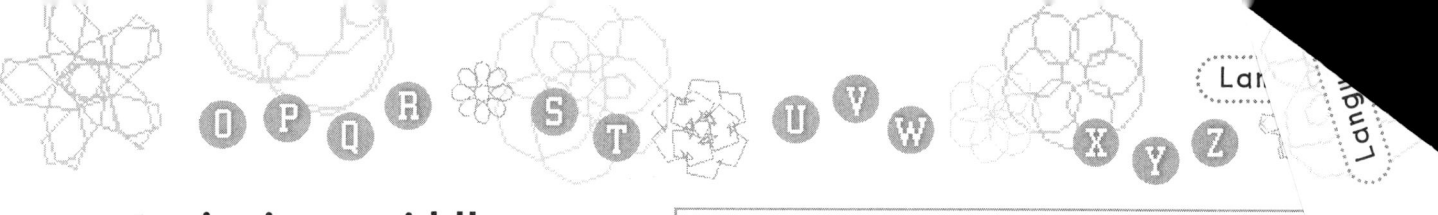

Beginnings, Middles, and Endings

Strengthen students' abilities to recognize letters, and blend the sounds they make to create words, with this activity. Create a three-column template for sorting stamps by beginning, middle, and ending sounds. For example, with the word CAT, place the letter C in column 1, the letter A in column 2, and the letter T in column 3. Have children stamp pictures that represent the beginning, middle, and ending sounds in this word in the appropriate columns. For example, under C they might stamp *cat*, *cow*, and *carrot*. Under A they might stamp *apple*, *bat*, and *man*. Under T they might stamp *tiger*, *plant*, and *pet*. To save time, make up a set of these templates in advance and store them in a Kid Pix folder. Label the templates so that students can easily pick the ones they want.

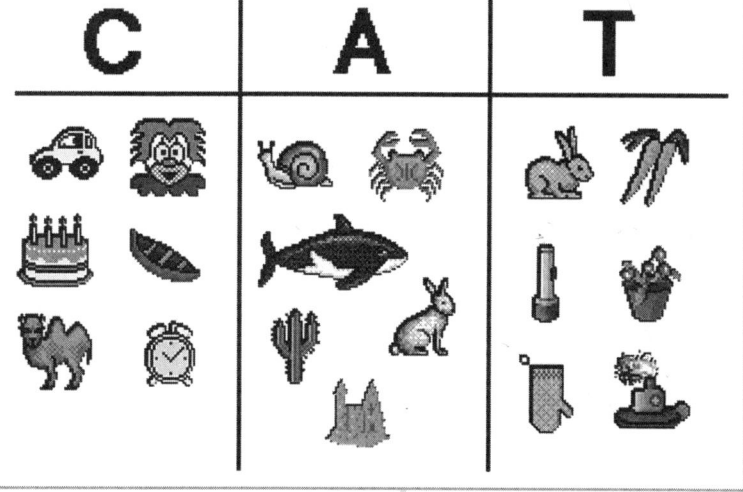

Charlotte Sassman and Regina Woods
Alice Carlson Applied Learning Center
Fort Worth, Texas

You may also specify that students stamp pictures that start with the corresponding sounds. For the *a* in *cat*, then, they might stamp pictures for words that also have the same middle sound (a), such as *pan*, *crab*, and *hat*.

Silly Sentences

When students select the DRAWME option (from the GOODIES menu), they can see and hear silly sentences—for example, "I'm a laughing volcano with a hundred toes and a pickle in my nose and boy oh boy, am I hungry!" The sentence is spoken one phrase at a time and stays on the screen. These silly sentences make great story starters.

- Have students choose DRAWME and use the TYPE TEXT tool to add on to the sentence that appears.
- Have students use the WACKY PENCIL, WACKY BRUSH, or RUBBER STAMP tools to illustrate the silly story.
- Students can share their stories by saving the pages in a slide show (each child can contribute a Silly Sentences slide) or by printing out pages to make a class book.

Lynn Foust
Emily Dickinson School
Bozeman, Montana

Sound Advice

Most newer computers give you the ability to record sound. Kid Pix supports this with its RECORD feature. Recording sound messages on Kid Pix pages is a useful option, especially for young children in the early stages of reading. For example, recording the question on the Hide-and-Seek Alphabet Book activity page will let beginning readers work independently.

Hide-and-Seek Alphabet Book

Reinforce letter recognition by creating alphabet hide-and-seek games with the COLORME pictures in the GOODIES menu.

- Open a COLORME picture. Use stamps to add to the picture, choosing those that reinforce a particular letter represented in the picture.
- Use the TEXT tool or TYPE TEXT option to add a question, such as: *How many things can you find that start with the letter B?* If your computer has recording capabilities, record the question as a sound message.

Martine Wayman
Kenmore Elementary School
Kenmore, Washington

My Own Letterhead

Encourage writing (and the art of letter writing) by having students make personalized letterheads. Have children follow these basic steps to get started. Store children's letterheads in a file (labeled by name) to make it easy for them to make additional copies.

- Use the TYPE TEXT option or TEXT tool to type in your name.
- Choose a picture from the stamp collection. Try to choose one that says something about you. For example, if you collect model airplanes, you can repeat an airplane stamp across the top of the page. (Hold down the mouse button and move the stamp across the page.) Or, use the WACKY PENCIL to draw a picture that says something about you.
- Go to the EDIT menu and select SAVE AS. Give your page a name. Print a test copy and make adjustments. Then print clean copies for letter writing.

Poem Builders

These poetry starter pages let children collaborate on *list poems*—a simple but rewarding form for young children. List poems are basically lists of words or phrases related to a topic. Mary O'Neill's "Sound of Water" (from *What Is That Sound?* by Mary O'Neill) is a favorite poem that follows this format. It begins, "The sound of water is: Rain, Lap, Fold, Slap…" Each line is a new word for the sound of rain. To set up list poems for your students to continue, follow these steps.

- Open a new page.
- Use the TYPE TEXT option to type in a poetry starter—for example, *The color red is:*
- Use the TYPE TEXT option to type a word for something that is red—for example, *strawberry*. Stamp or draw a picture of a strawberry.
- Have children continue, adding to the poem with their own words and pictures. (When children reach the end of the first page, open a new page to add on.)
- Print out the completed poem. Read the poem aloud, letting children recite their own lines.

Variation: Have children create a new page for each line of the poem. Instead of using stamps, have them draw pictures to illustrate the words. Print and bind pages to make a picture-book poem. Let children take turns bringing the book home to share with families. Or, make a class set of each page and collate to make individual copies.

Sizing Up Stamps

To enlarge stamps, use the SHIFT and CONTROL keys if you use Windows, or the SHIFT and OPTION keys if you use Macintosh.

Language Arts

Assessment Tool

How-to books make terrific assessment tools. For example, if you're doing a plant unit, children can create books to show how to plant a seed. In math, children can write how-to books to show how they solved a problem.

How-To Book List

- how to ride a bike
- how to make a paper airplane
- how to build a Lego machine
- how to draw a cat
- how to learn your spelling words
- how to build a tall block tower
- how to take care of a pet fish

How-To Books

From how to make a peanut butter sandwich to how to find a hidden treasure, there are endless opportunities for making how-to books with Kid Pix. How-to books let children practice sequencing skills in a meaningful way. Start by brainstorming ideas for how-to books. (See How-To Book List.) You might post these ideas near the computer so that children can access them easily.

Next, demonstrate the process by making a how-to book with the class. Choose a topic. Choose NEW to create a picture and write and record a sentence for the first step. Have a volunteer do the same for step two. Continue, creating new pages for each step. Go back and follow each step in order to see if anything has been left out, then make necessary revisions. Print each page to make the how-to book. Have children follow the same process to create their own how-to books. As a variation, students can save their pages as slides.

Lynn Foust
Emily Dickinson School
Bozeman, Montana

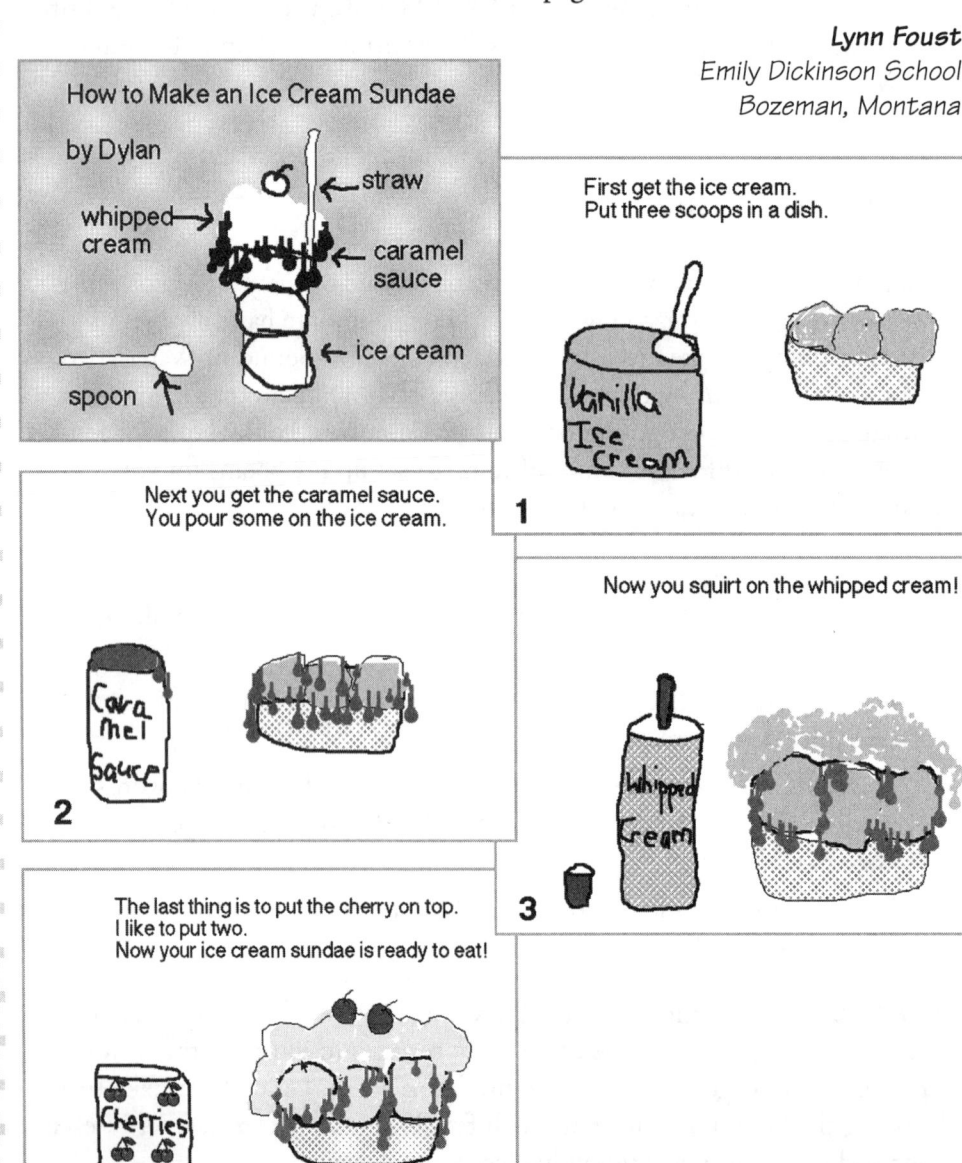

First, Next, Then, Finally

Help children strengthen sequencing skills with this activity. Use the LINE tool to divide a page into four equal parts. Leave a space at the top for children's names. Label the top left box "First," the top right "Next," the bottom left "Then," and the bottom right "Finally." Save the storyboard as a template. After sharing a story, have children use the template to retell the story in sequence, using the TYPE TEXT option to add words and the RUBBER STAMP, WACKY PENCIL, and WACKY BRUSH tools to add pictures. To go further, have children create additional pages to provide more detail in their retellings. They can use the pages to put together slide shows that retell the story from beginning to end.

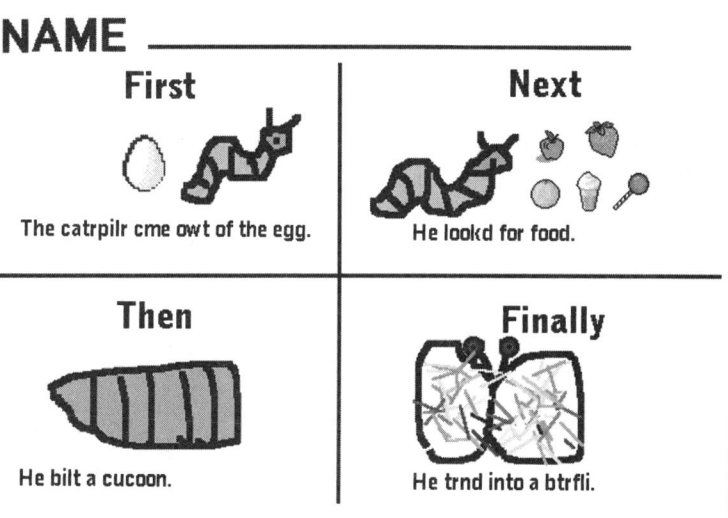

Mini Word Walls

Learning phonograms (also called *word families*), such as the *-ake* in *snake*, helps children more quickly read and write new words. For example, knowing the letters *-ake* in *snake* can also help children read and write *cake*, *Jake*, *lake*, and *make*. Create Kid Pix mini word walls to introduce chunks and give children a chance to explore them.

- Start by opening a new page. Use the TEXT tool or TYPE TEXT option to write the letters of the chunk at the top of the page. Use a large, bold font for this to set the chunk apart. Or, use the LINE tool to draw a box around it.

- Help children get started by adding a word that uses the specified chunk. For example, if the chunk is *-oat*, type the word *boat*. Stamp a picture of the word for beginning readers who need help reading the word.

- Invite children to add to the chunking pages you create by typing words that have the same chunk and stamping or drawing pictures to go with their words.

- Take time to revisit the mini word walls. You might let children take turns reading their words aloud. Cables are available to hook your computer up to a TV so that the whole class can easily see the screen. Or, print out and enlarge the pages and display them on a wall.

Tip

Finding Word Families

Familiar children's rhymes are an excellent source of word families in context. Stories and other reading material you share are also good sources. If you preview the material, you can look for phonograms that appear often, and ask children to listen for that sound in the words you read. (If you read the material a second time, ask children to clap or wave when they hear the sound.)

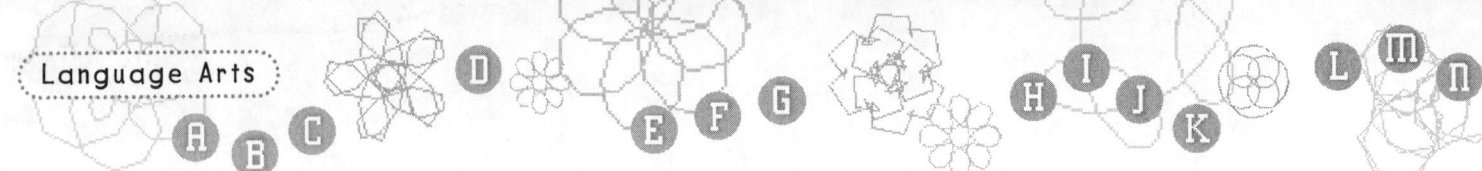

Language Arts

Tip

Slide Show Stories

You can save children's Silly Sally pages as a slide show, too. (You can include up to 99 pictures in one slide show, so there's plenty of room for everyone's work.)

Silly Sally Story Maker

Audrey Wood's *Silly Sally* (Harcourt Brace, 1992) is a favorite with children. In this cumulative rhyme, Silly Sally goes to town and meets all sorts of animals along the way. Use the story as a model for students' own silly stories. Start by sharing and discussing the story. Then let children use Kid Pix to write and illustrate a page for a class Silly Sally book.

- Open a new Kid Pix page.
- Create a Silly Sally template. Use the TYPE TEXT tool to type the words:

    Silly Sally went to town,
    Walking backwards upside down.
    On the way she met _____.

- Have children copy the page and use the TEXT tool to complete the story. Have them use the WACKY PENCIL, BRUSH, or RUBBER STAMP tools to illustrate the story, keeping the "silly" part of the story in mind.
- Have children type their name on their page and print.

Put children's pages together to make a class book. Read the story together, letting children take turns reading their pages. Set up a rotatation schedule so that children can share their story at home, too.

Marilee Schuhrke
John V. Leigh School
Norridge, Illinois

Language Arts

Memory Books

With school photos and Kid Pix, your students can create keepsake memory books they'll revisit again and again. Start by importing each child's photo into Kid Pix. Save photos on children's floppy disks (or in a file on the hard drive). Have children follow these steps to make their memory books.

- Insert your floppy disk into the disk drive and open it. Open Kid Pix. Select OPEN in the EDIT menu. Select the picture, and it will appear in the Kid Pix page.
- Use the magnet (in the MOVING VAN tool) to place your picture where you want it. Use the magnet to resize the picture, too.
- Give your memory book a name. Use the TEXT tool or TYPE TEXT option to write the title. Use the WACKY PENCIL, WACKY PAINT, and RUBBER STAMP tools to add decorations. This will be the cover of your memory book. Go to EDIT and select SAVE.
- Open a new Kid Pix page to make your first memory book page. Use words and pictures to tell about something special at school. Projects, field trips, visitors, and favorite books are just some of the things you can include in your memory book.
- Add more pages to your memory book. Save each page in a file labeled with your name and the project.

To help students include a range of memorable events from the year, you might make weekly suggestions and post them at the computer center. At the end of the year, help children print and bind their pages to make memory books. (To save time at the end of the year, you might print pages periodically, saving them in Memory Book file folders.)

Catherine Daly
Oak School
Hinsdale, Illinois

Tip

Picture Page Projects

In addition to making memory books, children can use their photo pages for many other projects during the year, such as autobiographies and thank-you notes.

Picture the Meaning

Help students to distinguish *literal* (stated) from *figurative* (suggested or implied) language in literature and writing with an activity that combines art, technology, and language arts.

- Introduce the idea of figurative language. Share an example, such as "Keep it under your hat." Let students suggest other examples. Record them on chart paper or the chalkboard. Invite children to explain or demonstrate what the various phrases would mean if taken literally. Let them tell what is really meant by each phrase.
- Let children choose phrases to illustrate in Kid Pix. Have them label their pictures with the phrases they depict. Print and display the pictures or combine them in a Kid Pix slide show.

Margaret Rappe
Jordan Community School
Chicago, Illinois

Six Little Ducks

"Six little ducks went swimming one day, over the pond and far away. Mother Duck said, 'Quack, quack, quack.' And five little ducks came swimming back…" This traditional verse is a favorite for teaching counting and subtraction skills.

- Write the verse "Six Little Ducks" on chart paper. Read it aloud with the class.
- Ask students to think about how they could illustrate the poem with number sentences.
- Open a Kid Pix page. Use the TYPE TEXT option to type the rhyme on the page. Leave room for a drawing and number sentence.
- Have children take turns making a copy of the page and illustrating it. They might use the WACKY PENCIL tool to add a wavy blue line for water, then stamp ducks from the NATURE and TEENYTOONS stamp sets (in the GOODIES menu).
- Have students use the TEXT tool to write a number sentence to go with the picture, such as 6 − 1 = 5.
- Let children continue, using new pages to add on to the verse. ("Five little ducks went swimming one day…four little ducks came swimming back.")

Marilee Schuhrke
John V. Leigh School
Norridge, Illinois

Tip

Flipping Stamps

To get the ducks facing opposite directions, children can use the EDIT STAMP tool in the TOOLBOX menu. They can flip the stamp from left to right or right to left. Other options include rotating the stamp.

Greater Than, Less Than, Equal To

Strengthen number sense by having children create two columns of numbers in Kid Pix. (Have them be sure to leave space between the columns.) Have them look at each set of neighboring numbers (left and right column) and decide if the first number is greater than, less than, or equal to the second number. They can then use the TYPEWRITER tool to insert their answers (> < =). Children greatly appreciate the escape from their workbooks on activities such as this!

Catherine De Gloria
Hillside Grade School
New Hyde Park, New York

Math

Math Fact Match

You can adapt this card-matching game to reinforce addition, subtraction, multiplication, or counting skills.

- Open a new Kid Pix page. Use the LINE tool to divide the page into an even number of "cards." (Eight works well.) Repeat this to make two identical pages of blank cards.

- To make an addition game, use the TEXT tool or TYPE TEXT option to fill in number sentences on one set of cards, one problem per card (such as 3 + 5, 8 + 4, 5 + 5, and so on). Type answers to the addition problems on the second set of cards, one answer per card.

- Print the cards, cut them apart, and mix them up. (You may wish to laminate cards for durability first.)

- Lay the cards face down on a table. Let children take turns turning over two cards. If the cards match (addition problem/answer), the player keeps the cards. Cards that don't match get turned over, and the next player takes a turn.

Tip

Click on Color

To add a background color to the dice, use the PAINT CAN tool.

Roll It! Add It!

Children can use the ROLL-THE-DICE option in the WACKY BRUSH tool for fun reinforcement of math skills.

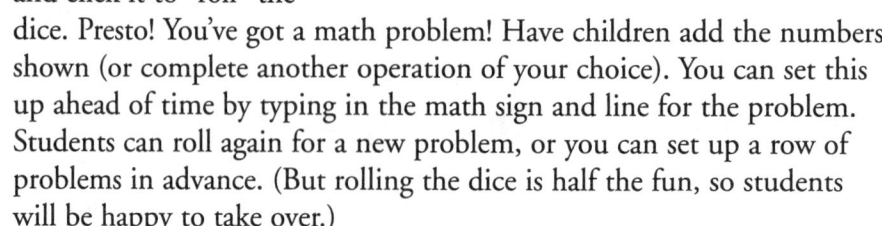

- Open a Kid Pix page.

- Click on the WACKY BRUSH tool. Select ROLL-THE-DICE and click it to "roll" the dice. Presto! You've got a math problem! Have children add the numbers shown (or complete another operation of your choice). You can set this up ahead of time by typing in the math sign and line for the problem. Students can roll again for a new problem, or you can set up a row of problems in advance. (But rolling the dice is half the fun, so students will be happy to take over.)

- As a variation, students can roll the dice to make math problem pages to trade with one another. Or, two students working at the computer together can take turns rolling and solving.

Jane Peterson
Nipomo Elementary School
Nipomo, California

Math Fact Bingo

With this Bingo game board you can make math games to reinforce each new skill you teach.

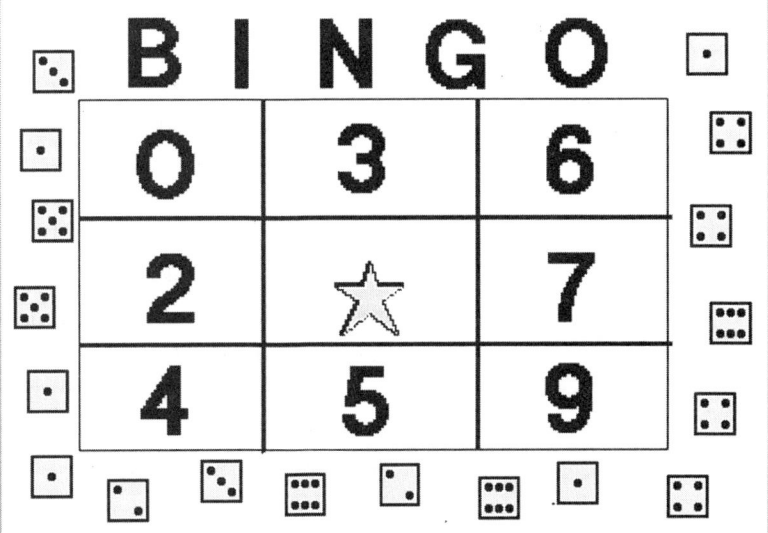

- Open a new Kid Pix page.
- Use the LINE tool to divide the page into a grid, three across and three down, as shown. Use the RUBBER STAMP tool to make a border.
- Make a copy of the blank Bingo board. Decide which math skill you want to reinforce and fill in each square with a number that represents a possible answer. For example, if you are teaching addition of numbers to 10, choose numbers in the 0 to 20 range. Stamp a star (or other picture) in the center space. This is a "free" space.
- Make a class set of the game board, varying each one by changing the positions of the numbers. (Each child will have a slightly different board.)
- Make a set of number-sentence strips to reinforce the skill. You can rearrange the order of addends, for example, including both 8 + 4 and 4 + 8. To make these with Kid Pix, use the LINE tool to divide the page down the middle. Draw lines across to create one-inch strips. Use the TEXT tool to write the number sentences on the slips. Print and cut apart.
- Place the number sentences in a bag or box. To play, give each child a game board and markers. (You can use chips, pennies, dried beans, etc.) Randomly select number sentences and read them aloud. Have children determine the solution and see if they have that number on their boards. If so, have them place a marker on that space, with the goal being to fill a line across, down, or diagonally.
- Use the same game board template to cover other math skills, such as subtraction and multiplication. Just open the template, and repeat the steps above to create a new set of boards and number-sentence strips. You can provide additional practice by inviting children to make and share their own math Bingo games. They'll have fun leading classmates in the games they make.

Variation: For a twist, switch the game around. Put the number sentences on the game boards and the numbers on the strips of paper. Call out a number to see if children can find a matching number sentence.

Stamp That Math!

For practice with operations, use Kid Pix to create number sentences and word problems, both enhanced by stamps.

Number Sentences: Use the RUBBER STAMP tool to stamp addition or subtraction picture problems and let children stamp out answers. You can also let children stamp the number that corresponds to each part of the number sentence, or you can do this yourself.

Word Problems: Make rebus math problems, using stamps in place of some words. Children will enjoy making their own rebus math problems to share, too. You might set up a surprise rebus problem each day, storing it in a folder for children to open and solve.

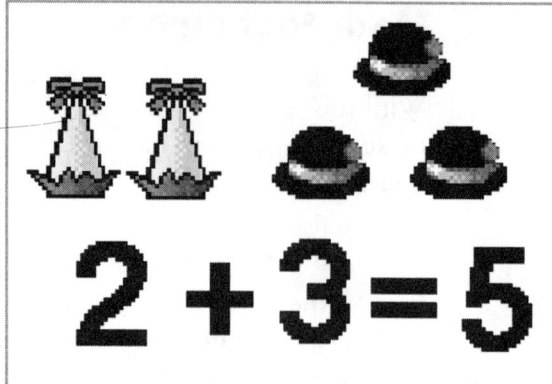

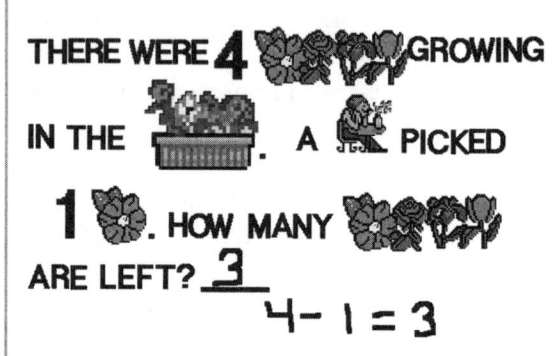

Linda Kennedy
Sleepy Hollow School
Orinda, California

100 Days Poster

Combine math, technology, and language arts skills in a simple activity that celebrates 100 days of school. Have children open a new Kid Pix page and write a number problem, the answer to which is 100. Have them use stamps to represent the number problem. Let children print their pages and display on a wall outside the classroom, gallery style. Give children time to browse the "math gallery" and see what their classmates came up with!

Bonnie Olinto
Bitburg Elementary School
Bitburg Air Base, Germany

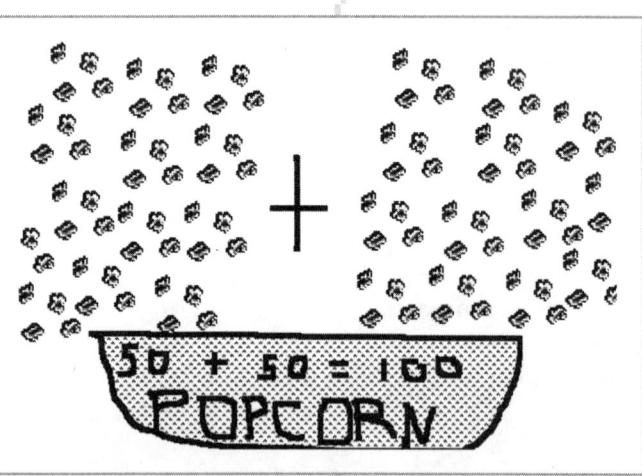

Arrays for Math! Quilt

Children develop a foundation for learning multiplication facts by working with arrays. Here's how to use Kid Pix to make an array-filled quilt.

- ☼ Open a new Kid Pix page.
- ☼ Use the RUBBER STAMP tool to stamp pictures in an array—for example, two rows of three. Beneath the array, write a multiplication sentence that goes with the array: 2 x 3 = 6. Write several other multiplication sentences on the page, and let children create arrays that go with them.
- ☼ Let children use the RUBBER STAMP tool to create arrays on new pages and use the TEXT tool to stamp the number sentences that go with them. Or, pair up children. Have them take turns creating the arrays and writing the sentences.
- ☼ Have children arrange their arrays on a large sheet of bulletin board paper, leaving an inch or so between each array. Glue arrays in place, then add strips of colorful paper between the arrays for a quilt-like effect.

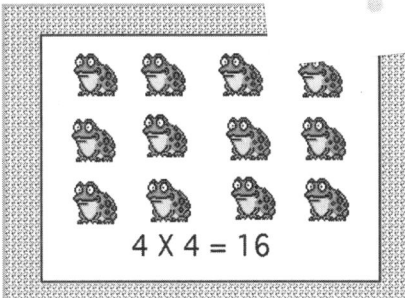

Catherine Daly
Oak School
Hinsdale, Illinois

Dot to Dot

The WACKY BRUSH tool features an option for making dot-to-dot pictures, which automatically numbers points as you draw. When you're finished with the picture, release the mouse and the connecting lines will disappear, leaving only the numbered dots. To make dot-to-dot pictures that reinforce number patterns, use the WACKY PENCIL or BRUSH to make an outline of a picture with dots. Use the TEXT stamp or TYPE TEXT tool to number the dots. For example, to teach counting by twos, number the dots 2, 4, 6, 8, 10, and so on. Save the page as a template. Have children make a copy, then use the WACKY PENCIL to connect the dots.

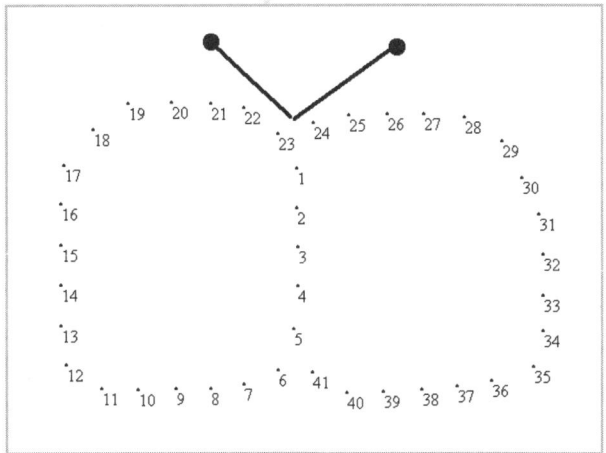

Debbie Hill
Emily Dickinson School
Bozeman, Montana

Show It With Stamps

Children develop number sense in different ways every day—for example, noticing how many, how much, how tall, or how long. One way to reinforce number sense with Kid Pix is to simply type numbers on pages (one per page), and have children use the RUBBER STAMP tool to stamp the corresponding number of objects. They can use the TEXT tool to write words for the numbers, too (for example, one rainbow, two ducks, three stars, and so on). Try the same thing to reinforce counting by twos, fives, etc. Let children print their pages and staple to make counting books. Students will have fun sharing their books with one another and noticing how many different ways they all showed the same numbers.

Variations: Reinforce number sense in other ways, too—for example, by exploring different ways to write sums. On the first page, type a number. Add a sound message asking children to write as many number sentences as they can to show that number. Have them stamp pictures on the pages to represent the number sentences, too. For example, for the number 5, children might type 1 + 1 + 1 + 1 + 1; 2 + 3; 4 + 1; 2 + 1 + 2; and 0 + 5, and then stamp pictures for each.

Roll and Graph

Children may be familiar with a math activity that asks them to guess the probability of rolling each number on a die out of some predetermined number of rolls. With Kid Pix, they can do this activity on the computer, graphing results as they go.

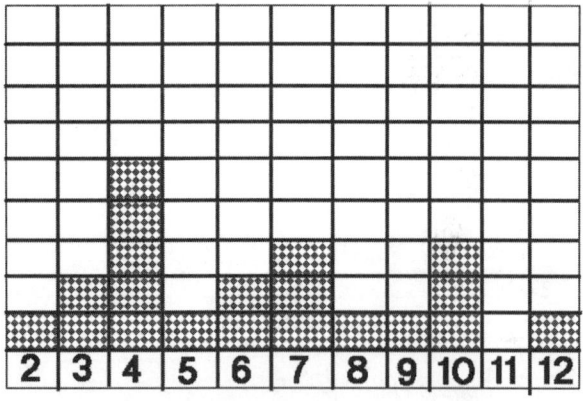

- Set up a template for the activity, using the LINE tool to create a graph as shown.
- Have children select the WACKY BRUSH tool and choose the ROLL-THE-DICE option.
- Have them roll the dice ten times, "pouring" paint on the graph to show the result of each roll.
- Have children print their graphs and compare results.

Margaret Kolnik
San Marcos Elementary School
Chandler, Arizona

Send-Home Calendar

This class calendar gives children practice with real-life math skills and keeps parents informed about school news. Divide children into teams, one for each month of the school year. Have each team select a month for which to research holidays, school events, birthdays, and so on. (You might brainstorm the kinds of information students will include on the calendars and post the list for easy reference.) When children have gathered their information, have them decide on a picture to illustrate the calendar page. Children preparing a calendar for February, for example, might draw pictures to celebrate Black History Month. When children are ready to prepare their calendar pages, guide them in following these steps.

- Use the LINE tool to create a 7 by 5 grid, leaving about 1 1/2 inches at the top.
- Use the TEXT tool to write the month, year, and days of the week at the top.
- Use the TEXT tool to number each square in the grid. (Check to make sure students know on which day the month starts.)
- Use the TYPE TEXT option to add information about holidays, birthdays, and so on.
- Open a new Kid Pix page. Use the WACKY PENCIL, WACKY BRUSH, and RUBBER STAMP tools to make pictures that correspond to the month. Have children use the RECTANGLE tool to make a box on each picture page. Use this space to share classroom news with parents, such as tips for learning at home and information about upcoming trips.
- Print both pages for each month. Make a class set, collate, and bind.

Tama Bruder
P.S. 231 at 212
Brooklyn, New York

Tip

One Month at a Time

Rather than try to complete the entire calendar at once, you might schedule teams for the year, then a week or so before each new month begins, have children create their calendar pages to send home.

Big, Bigger, Biggest!

Use Kid Pix rubber stamps to reinforce the math concepts of *big, bigger, biggest* in this book-based activity. Start by sharing *Who Can Boo the Loudest?* by Harriet Ziefert (HarperCollins, 1990), a Halloween story in which two ghosts compete to frighten the moon. Discuss the three sizes or sounds: *big, bigger, biggest*. Open a Kid Pix picture, click on the RUBBER STAMP tool, and pick a stamp. Stamp the picture on the page, then demonstrate how to make the stamp bigger. (See page 8.) Then make it even bigger. Use the TEXT tool or TYPE TEXT option in the EDIT menu to label each picture: *big, bigger, biggest*. Let children take turns making and labeling their own big, bigger, biggest stamp pictures.

Rhonda Turner
J. O. Schulze Elementary School
Irving, Texas

Tip

Simplify the Steps

For younger children, make a Big, Bigger, Biggest template, typing the words on the page for them. Have children copy the template, then choose stamps to illustrate the concepts *big, bigger, and biggest*. This is a good opportunity to introduce the keyboard commands used to resize stamps. (See page 8.)

Sorting Stamps

Sorting and classifying is a skill that students use across the curriculum. Though Kid Pix stamps are already sorted into categories for ease of use, you can create new categories to challenge children's sorting skills.

- Divide a page into three columns. Label each column with your sorting criteria, such as People, Animals, Food.
- Have children choose stamps that fit into each category and stamp them in the appropriate categories.
- For a challenge, give children a blank sorting template and challenge them to find new ways to sort a set of stamps. (This could be as simple as "Stamps I Love" and "Other Stamps.")

Charlotte Sassman and Regina Woods
Alice Carlson Applied Learning Center
Fort Worth, Texas

Pick a Pattern

Reinforce patterning skills by using the RUBBER STAMP tool to make pattern starters for children to continue.

- Open a new page.
- Create a pattern with stamps, letters, numbers, or symbols. For example, make a simple AB pattern by alternating a star and a heart. Make more challenging patterns by introducing more stamps.
- Go to the EDIT menu and select SAVE AS to save the pattern starter. Give the pattern starter a name and click SAVE.
- Have children complete patterns by using the appropriate stamps, letters, numbers, or symbols.

Store pattern starters in a labeled folder so that students can easily choose patterns to complete. If you make patterns in varying levels of difficulty, set up different folders for storing them, labeled to indicate the level—for example Pattern Starters 1, Pattern Starters 2, Pattern Starters 3 (with one being the easiest, three the most difficult). Show students how to make a copy of the pattern page before getting started. That way, your folders will remain stocked. Keep the activity fresh by periodically adding new patterns.

Variation: Set up an extra folder for patterns students make themselves and want to share.

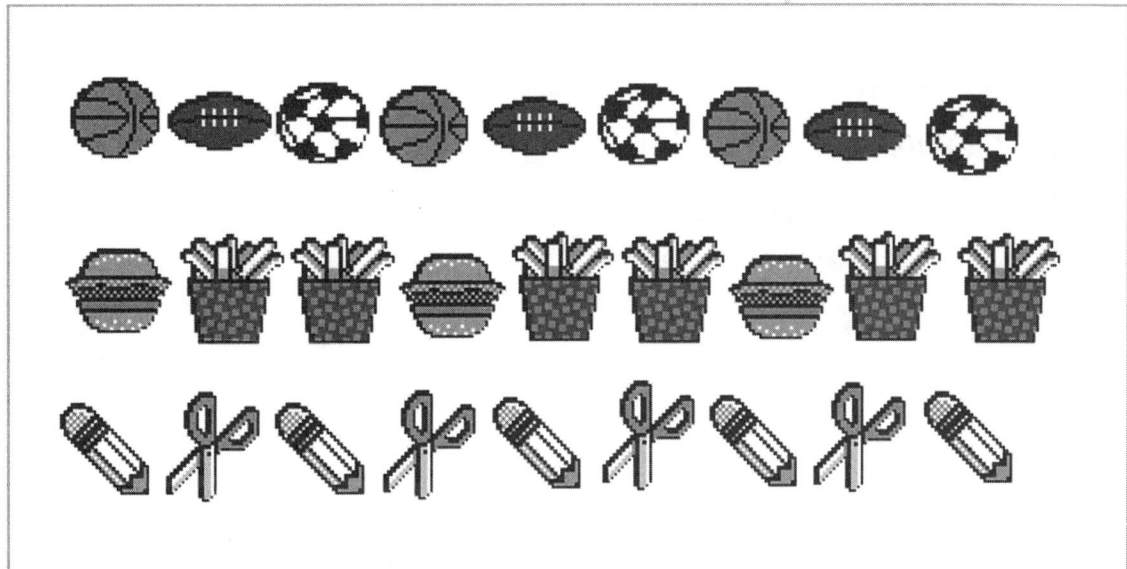

Math

Tip

For Upper Grades

If you complete this project with older students, arrange opportunities for them to share their books with younger children. For suggested number books, check *Irresistible 1, 2, 3s* by Joan Novelli (Scholastic Professional Books, 2000). Try the same activity to reinforce letter recognition. See *Irresistible A, B, Cs* (Scholastic Professional Books, 2000) for favorite alphabet books to share.

Creative Counting Books

Some of the most appealing books for children are number books. Simply written and often strikingly illustrated, these books invite children to make mathematical connections from page to page. This activity builds on those books, challenging students to create their own number books and, in the process, stretch their imaginations as well as their understanding of concepts.

- Collect and display a variety of number books for your class to study. (See Tip, left.) Discuss how the illustrators handled the task of teaching about numbers. Look at the ways they used color and other design features.
- Divide the class into groups. Each group will produce a number book. Have students in each group meet to decide on a general theme for the book. This theme could relate to subject matter the class is studying, such as an ocean number book.
- Have each group divide up the work, with each member responsible for designing and creating a certain number of pages.
- Have students use Kid Pix tools to create pictures and text for their books, then print out the pages and bind them together in a book.

Martine Wayman
Kenmore Elementary School
Kenmore, Washington

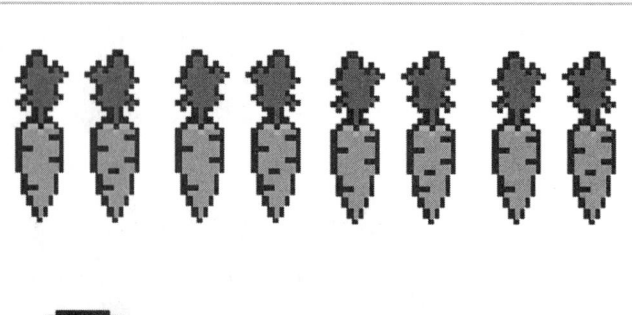

Line Art

Introduce the math terms *horizontal* and *vertical* by exploring the art of Mondrian. Then let children learn more about lines by creating their own Mondrian-style art with Kid Pix.

- Share prints by Mondrian (see Tip, right) and discuss his use of line. Introduce the words *horizontal* and *vertical* and let children find examples of each.

- To have children create their own Mondrian-style art, have them place two or three horizontal lines anywhere on the screen. (The lines should touch the edge of the screen.) Have them add two or three vertical lines. These lines can be anywhere—close together or far apart. These lines also need to touch the edge of the screen.

- Continue, having children add a couple of lines at a time. Then have children fill in the spaces between the lines using the PAINT BUCKET tool. You might have them notice the colors Mondrian used and choose similar colors for their paintings.

- Display children's art alongside samples of Mondrian's work. Invite them to notice similarities and differences.

Teresa Lisum
Emerson Elementary School
Warren, Ohio

Tip

Where to Find Prints

For links to web sites that feature the artwork of Piet Mondrian, go to www.artcyclopedia.com

Fish in a Lake

To give children practice in reading a chart, as well as in counting and problem solving, go fishing with Kid Pix!

- Create a chart showing how many red, blue, green, and yellow fish are in a lake.

- Give children a copy of the chart. (Or post it at the computer center with directions.)

- Have children open a new page and draw a picture of a lake. Have them use stamps or drawing tools to fill the lake with fish, according to the chart. They may want to use the CIRCLE and STRING tools to draw the fish and the COLOR PALETTE to select the correct colors.

- Have children write a sentence to go with their pictures to tell how many fish of each color are in the lake, as well as how many there are in all.

Judy Oleson
Deuel Elementary School
Clear Lake, South Dakota

Number Puzzles

These puzzles combine a little hide-and-seek with number fun. Use the COLORME option in the GOODIES menu to make number puzzles.

- Select a COLORME picture from the GOODIES menu. Use rubber stamps to add to the picture. (See sample, below.)

- Use the TEXT TOOL to add a caption that invites children to find and count objects—for example, *How many birds can you find in the picture? How many bicycles can you find in the picture? How many birds and bicycles are there in all?*

- Set up blanks for children to complete the number sentences at the bottom of the page.

- If your computer is equipped with a sound card and microphone, record the questions so that students can hear as well as read them.

- Let children open and copy the number puzzles, using the TEXT tool or TYPE TEXT option to complete the number sentences.

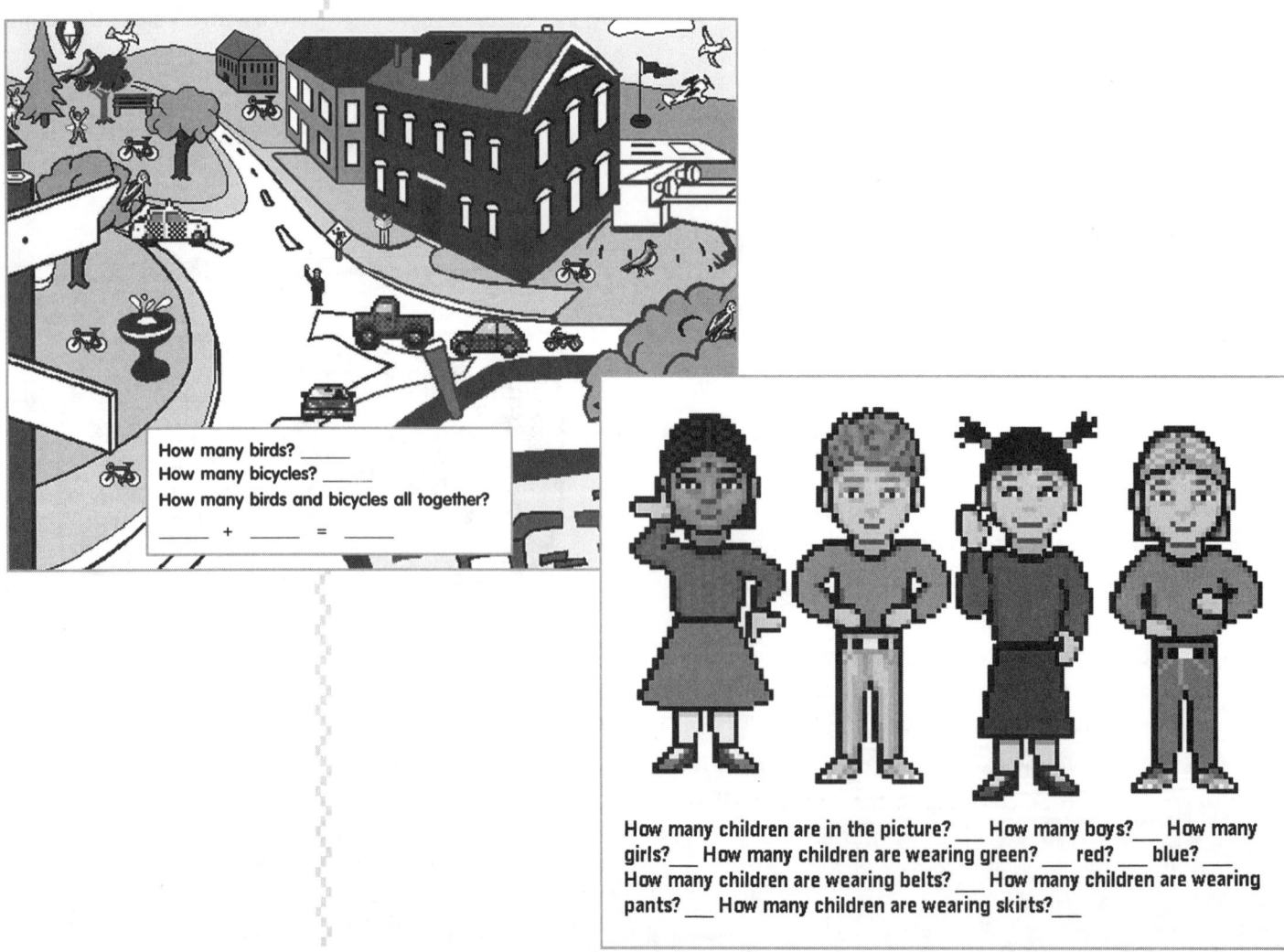

More Than, Less Than, Equal To

Set up a simple template on Kid Pix to reinforce concepts of more than, less than, and equal to. Students can complete it again and again to show what they know in different ways.

- Divide a page into three parts. Place the symbols for more than (>), less than (<), and equal to (=) in each section (one symbol per section).

- Let children use the stamps to demonstrate their understanding of each concept—for example, placing seven strawberry stamps to the left of the "more than" sign, and four pear stamps to the right of the sign.

Pat Scoggan
Butler School
Springfield, Illinois

Fraction Fun

Kid Pix slide shows turn learning about fractions into exciting productions. As part of your unit on fractions, ask each child to create one slide show frame that demonstrates a fraction. Have students illustrate and label the fraction, and write a sentence to go with it. Put the slide show together by adding a title and ending slide and transitions between frames. This slide show will give you and your students a look at the many ways we use fractions in our lives.

Kathleen Kuceyeski
Parkway Elementary
Alliance, Ohio

Tip

Try This, Too

For a variation, reverse the activity, stamping two groups of objects on the page and letting students fill in the <, >, or = sign to show the relationship between the two groups of objects.

Social Studies

Neighborhood Maps

Strengthen your students' map-reading skills with an activity that looks at your school neighborhood. Use the WACKY PENCIL tool to create a simple map, selecting the circle and rectangle options to make a space for pictures of each of the following captions:

- This is our school.
- This is to the left of our school.
- This is to the right of our school.
- This is behind our school.

Have children complete the map by drawing pictures or using stamps to show what is in front of, behind, to the left of, and to the right of the school. Though each child will be completing the same map, expect to see lots of variations. One child may see the house next door to the school, while another might see something entirely different, such as a tree where birds are nesting. Have children print their maps to share with the class. Discuss the many things that are part of your neighborhood. Use the discussion to reinforce words that show direction, such as *left, right, in front of,* and *behind.*

Go further by inviting children to use the template to make maps of their neighborhoods at home. Move from these simple maps to more complex maps—for example, mapping the street that the school is on in greater detail.

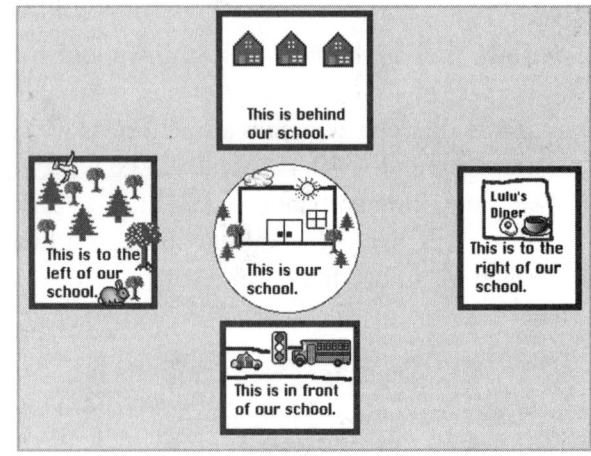

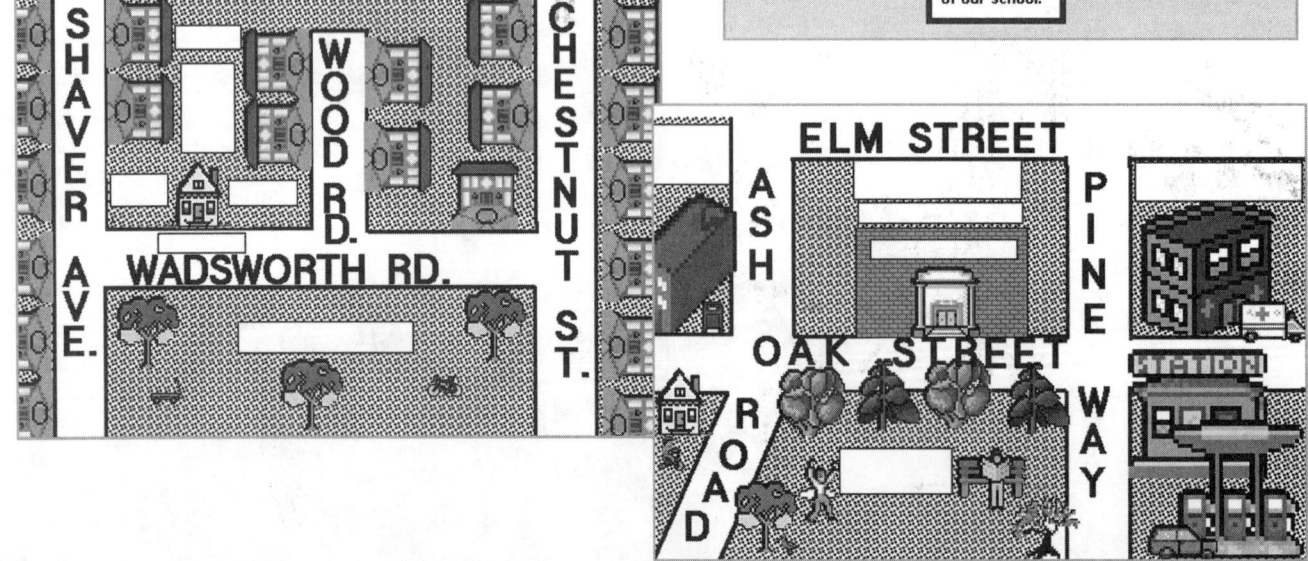

Social Studies

Transportation Sort and Stamp

As part of a unit on transportation, let children chart different ways to get around—for example, by land, water, and air. Have children use the LINE tool to set up a three-column chart. Have them sort through the RUBBER STAMPS looking for examples of each kind of transportation, then stamp them in the appropriate columns. Bring children together to display and discuss their charts. Use the information they gathered to learn more about the ways people get around. For example, ask:

- How can we group the different ways people get around on land? For example, some are powered by people (*bicycle, skateboard*), and others are powered by gasoline (*car, bus, taxi,* and so on).
- Of all the ways people get around in the air, which do you think is fastest? Why?
- How many land transportation vehicles have wheels?

Catherine De Gloria
Hillside Grade School
New Hyde Park, New York

Time Lines Tell Stories

Strengthen sequencing skills with time line slide shows that invite children to record memorable events in their lives.

- Open a new page.
- For the first entry (first page), have children use the TEXT tool or TYPE TEXT option to record their birth date. Have them use the WACKY PENCIL or BRUSH tools to draw a picture.
- Have children add additional pages to record other events in their lives—for example, the birth of a sibling, first stitches, first tooth lost, and the first day of kindergarten. For each page, have children create a picture for the event, and complete the sentence: *I was* [age.]
- Have children open the SLIDESHOW option and copy their pages into the MOVING VANS to make slides. Children can also print out the slides to make time line books.
- To take the activity further, have children write stories about specific events.

Debbie Hill
Emily Dickinson School
Bozeman, Montana

Story Structure

Use the time line activity as a way to discuss story structure—and the fact that many stories, like the ones on children's time lines, are told in *chronological order*. Invite children to think of stories they know that are written in chronological order—for example, biographies.

Social Studies

Fire Safety Week

Fire Safety Week is in October, but you can use this activity any time of the year to strengthen children's fire safety skills.

Fire Safety Map

Safety skills are an ongoing part of a primary curriculum. To reinforce fire safety skills, have students use the WACKY PENCIL, WACKY BRUSH, and LINE tools to draw a floor plan of their home. A list of things to include follows.

- the family's "safety spot"—an outside place family members agree to meet in case of a fire
- a safe-exit line from each room in the house to the "safety spot" outside
- yellow stickers to show smoke detector locations

Mount children's fire safety drawings on construction paper and have them dictate sentences about fire safety. (They can also use the TYPE TEXT tool to add these while in Kid Pix.) Send the maps home, encouraging families to talk about fire safety, practice fire drills together, and check smoke detectors. Repeat this activity throughout the year as a safety reminder. Compare early drawings with later ones to see how mapping skills have grown!

Fran Voss
Unity Point School
Carbondale, Illinois

Our State in a Slide Show

As students move beyond their communities to learn more about their state, have them put together a slide show of the facts they gather. Together, research important events and people in your state's history. You might include such information as the earliest people to settle in the state, significant events, crops, native animals and plants, state flag and flower, architecture, industry, famous people, and so on. Let children each choose a slide to create, then guide them in following these steps to complete the project.

- Have children prepare their text and pictures on regular Kid Pix pages. They can draw their own pictures, use stamps, or import pictures from other sources. (Children can use the Slide Show Organizer on page 62 to plan slides first.)

- Have children edit their pictures (text and art), then save them in a group folder. (Keeping the pictures together will make it easier for children to find them. Because you may have 20 or more slides, have children use their name when they save the pictures to make it easy to find the right one.)

- Together, decide the slide sequence.

- Open the SLIDESHOW option and then click on the SELECT button. (This is the first button on the bottom of the van.) The PICK A PICTURE! dialogue box will appear. Click on the name of the correct picture, then click on SELECT to load the picture into the slide show MOVING VAN.

- Continue, selecting each picture in order.

- When all pictures are loaded, go back to each and add finishing touches. Click on the PICK A SOUND! icon to add sounds. Click on the TIME SLIDER icon to set the amount of time that will elapse between slides. Click on the PICK A TRANSITION! icon to choose how the show will move from one slide to the next.

- Preview the slide show, keeping paper and pencil handy to make notes. Edit as necessary, then share your show with an audience.

Lynn Foust
Emily Dickinson School
Bozeman, Montana

Tip

Editing Slide Shows

Vroom! You can edit slide shows by driving moving vans from one location to another. Just click on the van and drag it to the new position. When you move a van to the position of a full moving van, that van will be bumped to the right, moving those after it to the right as well. If you leave an empty van behind, you can use CLEAN UP (in the GOODIES menu) to make it disappear. You can also leave an empty moving van as is—the program will skip right over it.

Social Studies

Tip

Story Starters

Images of familiar sights, such as community landmarks, are a terrific source of story starters. Using the images they enhance in "What Belongs Here?," have students write or dictate stories about places in their community. They can open new pages to tell their stories, or copy the pictures into the SLIDESHOW option and tell the stories on slides. Print out pages or slides to make books about your community. Have students make covers and give their books titles—for example, *All About the Bank* or *A Visit to the Farm*.

What Belongs Here?

Your students will delight in using digital images imported into Kid Pix to play "What Belongs Here?" As they learn about their community, they'll strengthen writing skills, including attention to detail.

- Prepare by taking digital photos of places in your community, such as the playground, the neighborhood, the grocery store, and the pet store. (You could also use a standard camera and scan in the photos, or ask your photo finisher to store the images on a floppy or CD-ROM or send them to you via the Internet.)
- Download the pictures onto a disk and make copies for each student.
- Have students choose images to import into Kid Pix and use stamps from the program to add details, showing what belongs in the scenes they've selected.
- Have students write or dictate sentences about their pictures. Use the RECORD option to record students reading their sentences, too.

Lorraine Leo
Jackson School
Newton, Massachusetts

Plains, Plateaus, Mountains, and More

For a unit on landforms, let children use Kid Pix to create pictures that incorporate mountains, valleys, deserts, peninsulas, lakes, rivers, plains, plateaus, and so on.

These can be silly or serious—the only requirement is that the picture show an understanding of the landforms. Have students use the TYPE TEXT option to add captions to their pictures, labeling and telling about the landforms they've included.

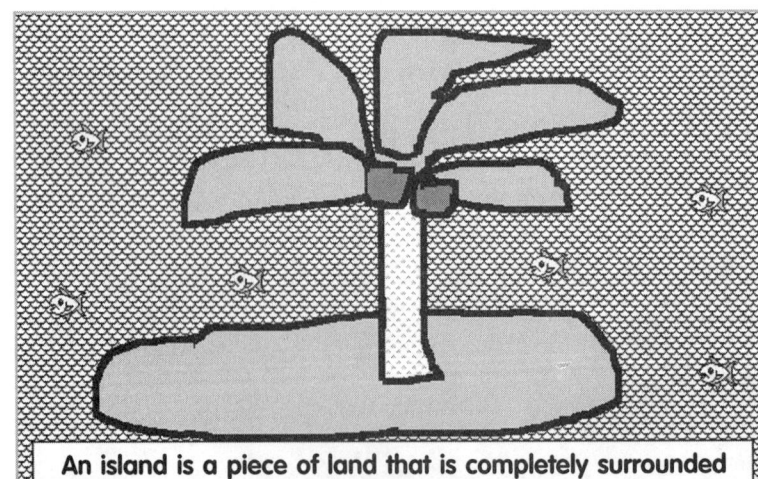

An island is a piece of land that is completely surrounded by water. The state of Hawaii is a group of islands.

Social Studies

Classroom Map-Makers

Support your geography curriculum with a map-making activity that strengthens spatial organization. Let children repeat the activity throughout the year to see how their mapping skills have grown.

- Ask students to pretend that the classroom has a glass ceiling. They're on top of the ceiling looking down into the classroom! What do they see? (This will help them gain a perspective on the entire room.)
- Have students sketch the room in preparation for making a map on Kid Pix. This will help them focus on the important elements of the room before creating a final map.
- Discuss directions—north, south, east, west. Label sections of the classroom to assist students with directionality as they make their maps.
- Have students create their maps with Kid Pix, using the pencil, paint, and stamp tools to show tables, chairs, meeting areas, the chalkboard, bulletin boards, dramatic play areas, bookshelves, and so on. Remind students to draw a compass rose on their maps first, and to use it to decide where things go.

Evelyn Sullivan
Williamstown Public Schools
Williamstown, Massachusetts

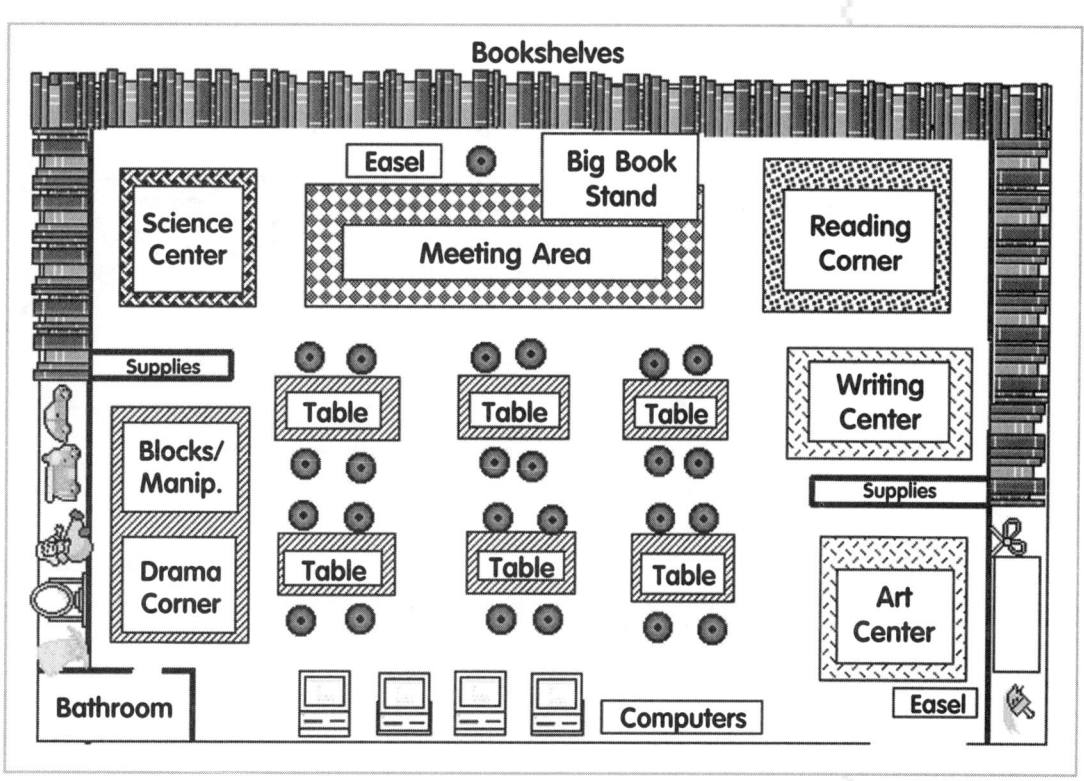

Social Studies

Stop and Go

How do rules help the children in your class get along? Invite students to share responses to this question, then ask: *What are some rules that help people get along in our community?* Discuss the role traffic lights play in helping people get along on the roads. (*They help people take turns at intersections, they help people avoid collisions,* and so on.) Review what each color in a traffic light stands for, then share the poem "Traffic Light" by Leland Jacobs.

Traffic Light

Sun up, sun down,
Day and night,
Demands are made
By the traffic light,
With colors
Red and green that glow.
Cars and people
Stop and go,
Obeying what
By day and night
Is ordered by the traffic light.

—by Leland Jacobs

Follow up by using Kid Pix to make a book about rules that help people get along.

- Open a new Kid Pix page.
- Demonstrate how to use various tools to write and illustrate a rule that helps people get along, such as "Pick up after yourself."
- Have children take turns creating new pages.
- Print pages and bind to make a book about getting along. You can also save pages in the SLIDESHOW option. Copy the slide show to a disk, selecting the STANDALONE option, to share with families.

Marilee Schuhrke
John V. Leigh School
Norridge, Illinois

Sharing School News

Turn everyday and special events at school into a slide show that will keep everyone informed about the day—from what's for lunch to who's having a special visitor. Students can use the program's text, painting, and drawing tools to create slides. They can also include digital photos, clip art, and so on. Any class that has access to Kid Pix can contribute slides to the show, making this a collaborative project that brings students across the grades together. (For more information on using the SLIDESHOW feature, see page 11.) You can run the slide show as a "stand alone" on a computer. (Select the SAVE AS STANDALONE option.) Or, run it as a continous loop on your school's video distribution system.

Lori Elliott
Phoenix Day School for the Deaf
Phoenix, Arizona

Tip

Open School Slide Show

Set up a computer or TV in the lobby or media center at open school nights. Run a school news slide show as a continuous loop to give families a look at a day in their children's lives.

Social Studies

Tip

More Games to Make

To make "What's My Capital" easier, include a picture of each state on the "capital" cards. This will help children identify matching cards. For variations on the matching game, try these ideas:

- Put state names on one set of cards and state shapes on another set of cards. Let children try to match shapes with names.
- Make state cards (shape and name) and matching state bird or flower cards.
- Learn more about the products each state is known for by making sets of cards to match state shapes and names with major products—for example, Oklahoma produces cattle, wheat, and oil.

What's My Capital?

Turn learning the states' capitals into a game.

- Open a new page and use the LINE tool to divide it into an even number of parts. (Eight works well.) Repeat this procedure to make additional pages.
- Write the name of each state on a card. Stamp a picture of the state on each card, too. Write the name of each state's capital on another set of cards. (You may also want to write the abbreviation for the state on this card.) Stamp a star on each card.
- Print each page and cut apart the cards. (You may wish to laminate them first.)
- Shuffle the cards and lay them face down on a table. Let children take turns choosing two cards to try to match a state and capital. If the cards match, the child takes them. If the cards do not match, they get turned over.
- When not in use, store cards in a reclosable sandwich bag.

Technology at Work

Your students might be surprised to learn that some children's book illustrators use computer drawing programs to color in their art. Here's a simplified look at how this happens.

- First, the illustrator makes pencil illustrations for the book and goes over the drawings with black marker.
- Next, the illustrator scans the images into a computer and saves them.
- Finally, the illustrator brings the pictures into a drawing program and colors them in.

Let students use Kid Pix to try the same technique. Have them make pencil drawings first, then go over the lines with black marker. Scan children's pictures and save them on individual disks. Have children bring their drawings into Kid Pix by opening the files. They can then use the WACKY PAINTBRUSH tools to color the pictures.

Follow up by talking about other ways people use computers in their work. Let children share ways they use computers in their work—for example, to communicate via e-mail, to research a project on the Internet, to edit and polish a piece of writing, and so on.

Catherine De Gloria
Hillside Grade School
New Hyde Park, New York

Social Studies

The Great Sphinx

Combine history and creativity with a lesson on ancient Egypt. Invite students to tell you what they know about the Sphinx. Share some history about this famous statue, as well as a picture of it. Guide students to notice the body of a lion and the head of a pharoah. Explain that archaeologists believe that the Egyptians thought this combination symbolized strength and wisdom. Follow up by letting students use Kid Pix to design statues of their own that symbolize something special to them. Guide them in following these steps.

- Use the WACKY PENCIL to draw a background. Fill in the background with the PAINT BUCKET.
- Click on the RUBBER STAMP and select an animal. Enlarge the animal using the Shift and Control keys. Stamp the animal on the background.
- Choose the head of a person and enlarge it. Stamp the head on top of the animal's head to create a statue.
- Add details to the picture using other stamps and tools.
- Use the TYPEWRITER tool to describe the new statue, giving it a name and telling what it symbolizes.

Karen Stuart
Westwind Elementary
Wolfforth, Texas

Social Studies

Slide-Show Biographies

Support lessons on famous people in history by making slide-show biographies. Kid Pix lets children combine facts and illustrations, as well as their recorded voices, to create impressive and informative (and manageable) presentations. You might plan a series of month-by-month slide-show biographies to take you from the start of the year to the end. For example, feature Johnny Appleseed in September and Shel Silverstein in October (born October 18). Students can use the slide-show biographies to present information on famous African Americans or presidents in February, and women in March.

Prepare for making the slide shows by gathering information about the person. List facts on chart paper and let each child choose one. Have children take turns using Kid Pix to create a slide show frame with their facts. Have them type in their facts, illustrate them, then record their voices to go with the slides. Add a title and closing page, choose transitions for getting from one frame to the next, and invite students to a screening! Make any adjustments, then share the slide show with an audience—for example, another class, visitors to the library, or family members on open school night.

Ann Molitor and Sandy Tunison
Ledgewood Elementary School
Rockford, Illinois

Johnny Appleseed loved the outdoors. He loved to take walks in the woods among the trees and flowers.

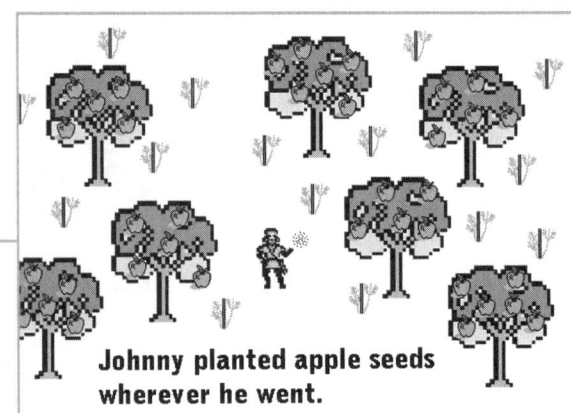

Johnny planted apple seeds wherever he went.

Johnny did not like fighting. He tried to help the Indians and settlers make peace.

Science in a Circle

You can adapt this graphic organizer to explore any science topic through literature. (See Read About Science, below.) *Corn Is Maize* by Aliki (HarperCollins, 1976) works well in fall, when many teachers weave harvest themes into lessons. In this fascinating story, children learn how the Native Americans cultivated the wild grass that is now an everyday part of our diets. Follow up by setting up a Kid Pix graphic organizer to let children demonstrate what they've learned.

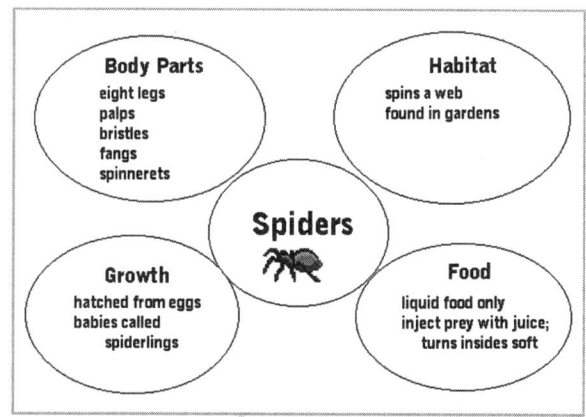

- Use the CIRCLE tool to make the graphic organizer. Add as many circles as you wish. Type the topic in the center circle.
- Complete the web as a class, using the TYPE TEXT option to add information to each surrounding circle.
- If you prefer, you can save the blank organizer as a template, and have children complete the webs independently or in pairs.

Rhonda Turner
J. O. Schulze Elementary School
Irving, Texas

Read About Science

Like *Corn Is Maize*, the following titles are just a sampling of the literature available to support favorite science topics at the primary level. Each lends itself to using graphic organizers such as the one shown above to let students demonstrate understanding.

HUMAN BODY: *Your Insides* by Joanna Cole (Putnam, 1992)

WEATHER: *Wild, Wet, and Windy* by Claire Llewellyn (Candlewick, 1998)

SEASONS: *Winter* by Ron Hirschi (Cobblehill, 1990) See other books in the series, too: *Fall, Spring, Summer.*

BEARS: *Looking at Bears* by Dorothy Hinshaw Patent (Holiday House, 1994)

SPACE: *So That's How the Moon Changes Shape* by Allan Fowler (Children's Press, 1991)

INSECTS: *Have You Seen Bugs?* by Joanne Oppenheim (Scholastic, 1998)

HABITATS: *Beaver at Long Pond* by William T. George and Lindsay Barrett George (HarperCollins Paperback, 2000)

PLANTS: *From Seed to Plant* by Gail Gibbons (Holiday House, 1991)

WHALES: *Big Blue Whale* by Nicola Davies (Candlewick, 1997)

Science

Postcards From Space

This simple interdisciplinary project can be adapted for any science topic, such as oceans or rain forests. Use it at any level, varying the amount of detail and text children include to make it easier or more challenging.

- Use the LINE tool to draw a postcard shape on the page. This will be the front of the postcard. Copy the shape to make the back of the postcard, and draw a line down the center of the back.

- Have children click on the RUBBER STAMP tool, then go to the GOODIES menu and select PICK A STAMP and SPACE. Have children use the stamps to make a picture of space on the front of the postcard. (They can also use the WACKY PENCIL and BRUSH tools.)

- On the left side of the back, have children use the TYPE TEXT option to compose a letter about space to a family member or friend. Remind children to include facts they've learned. Have them type in that person's name and address on the right side of the back.

- Print both sides of the postcard. Cut them apart and glue back sides together.

Anne LeFevre
Seeliger Elementary School
Carson City, Nevada

Dear Mom and Dad,
    Greetings from Space! Things are so different here! Instead of walking, we float because everything has no weight.
    I've been collecting moon rocks to bring home and show you. Wish you were here!
    Nigel

Mr. and Mrs. Ed Foster
604 County Rte. #4
Central Square, NY 13036

Collaborative Science Books

Whatever the science topic, students can show what they know by creating pages for a simple nonfiction book. For example, students studying penguins each created a page for a book by writing and illustrating a penguin fact. Bound together, students' pages make a wonderful nonfiction book to read aloud and share at the class library. Basic steps for making the books follow.

- Open a new page.
- Use the TEXT tool or TYPE TEXT option in the GOODIES menu to type a fact on the page.
- Use the WACKY PENCIL or WACKY BRUSH tool to illustrate the fact.
- Click on the RUBBER STAMP tool to add stamps to the picture.
- Save each page by selecting SAVE from the EDIT menu.
- Print each page by selecting PRINT from the EDIT menu.
- Bind pages together to make a book.

Variation: Have each child contribute an illustrated fact for a slide show. Older students might create an entire slide show themselves or with a partner. For example, as a culminating activity for an ocean unit, students can team up to create slide shows about different fish, combining a picture and fun fact to create each slide.

Donna Kurzinski
Washington Elementary
Mundelein, Illinois

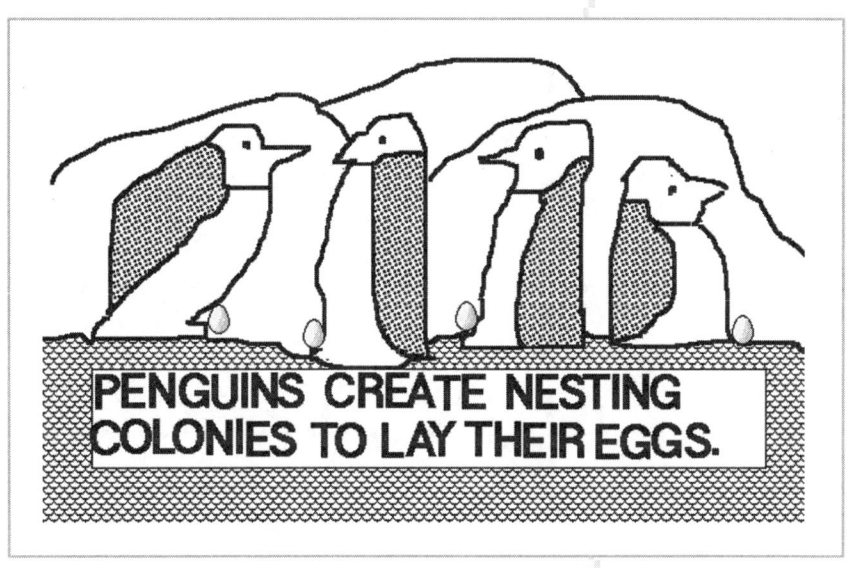

Science

Color It Cloudy

To make pictures for cloudy, partly cloudy, and snow, click on the CIRCLE tool. Change the color to blue. Use the solid circle to draw a cloud, the circle with dots for snow, and a combination solid and open circle for partly cloudy.

Stamp the Weather

As a class project, record weather for a month or more. Set up a calendar in Kid Pix for keeping track of the days and the weather conditions.

- Set up a calendar grid template with seven columns and five rows.
- Use the TEXT or ALPHABET STAMP tool to write the name of the month and the days of the week. Stamp the numbers for the days of the month in the boxes.
- Have children choose PICK A STAMP SET from the GOODIES menu, then click on the RUBBER STAMP tool. Have them select icons that correspond to possible weather conditions and stamp them at the bottom of the page, then use the TYPE TEXT tool to label the pictures.
- Each day, let a child record the weather on the calendar, stamping the appropriate picture in the space for that day.
- At the end of each week and month, count the number of days for each weather condition. Let children summarize the data in a report on the week or month's weather, summarizing the data.

Jeraldine Quesinberry
Dobson Elementary School
Dobson, North Carolina

Science

Closeup on Insects

For a unit about insects, take children on a walk around the school grounds. Have them look for insets in trees, bushes, in the grass, and under rocks. When you return to the classroom, make a list of all the insects children found. (An insect guidebook may be helpful.) Then let children follow these steps to record the experience in pictures, words, and sound.

- Open a new Kid Pix page. Select the PAINT CAN tool and click on the desired background color. Click on the screen to fill the page with this color.

- To add another large area of color, such as grass or dirt, select the PENCIL tool and the desired color, and draw the outline of the next area to be filled.

- Make sure to connect the ends of the outline or touch the ends of the line to each edge of the screen. (This will contain the color in the desired space.) Then select the PAINT CAN and the second color, and click in the area to be filled.

- Use the WACKY PENCIL to draw one of the insects. Choose a line thickness and pattern from the options bar below the picture, and then begin to draw. Change colors and line thicknesses as desired. (You may also use the WACKY BRUSH tool to vary the drawing. Select the paintbrush from the toolbar, and then select a style from the options bar below the picture.)

- Select the TEXT tool and click on letters shown to add a title for the drawing.

- To add sound—for example, the name of the insect and one fun fact—click on RECORD SOUND in the GOODIES menu. Click on the RECORD button and speak clearly. (There are 32 seconds available for recording.) When finished, click STOP and then SAVE.

- Print the picture. To omit the sound message, choose this option in PRINT.

Jennifer Prior
Edu-Prize School
Gilbert, Arizona

Tip

Adding Color

If you accidentally leave a break in the line that contains an area you are applying color to, the entire screen will fill with that color. If this happens, immediately click on the UNDO GUY and the previous screen will appear. Try again.

Science

Tip

More Slide Show Science

Children can create slide shows for almost any science topic. For example, after sharing *James and the Giant Peach* by Roald Dahl (Knopf, 1962), children can create slide shows about each of the insects in the story, including factual information on habitat, food, special characteristics, and so on.

To help children who are creating slide shows make the most of their time on the computer, use a slide-show organizer. (See page 62.) Have children complete one for each slide, including opening and closing slides.

Melissa Andrick Hughes
Nolley Elementary School
Akron, Ohio

Life-Cycle Shows

To wrap up an investigation of butterflies, have children create slide shows that depict the stages of a monarch's life cycle. In the process of developing Kid Pix science slide shows, students will accomplish numerous learning goals, including locating information and clarifying meaning, identifying main ideas and details, communicating knowledge of a topic, and demonstrating organization by developing a beginning, middle, and end. Naturally, their slide shows will be a good source of assessment information. The sample self-assessment checklist on page 63 lets students participate in assessment. Steps for a Life Cycles slide show follow. You can follow the same basic procedure for other science investigations. (See More Slide Show Science, left.)

- Have students gather and organize information about the life cycle of a butterfly from a variety of resources, such as multimedia encyclopedias, books, and students' science journals.
- Using Kid Pix drawing and painting tools, have students create pictures that show the stages of the life cycle.
- Using Kid Pix typing tools, have students add two facts to each picture.
- Have students create a title page for the slide show.
- Follow SLIDESHOW procedures to move pictures to slide show MOVING VANS.
- Add prerecorded sounds to slides as desired. (Or record facts in the picture-making stage.)
- Have students preview, then present, their slide shows.

Barb White
Latham Elementary School
Cottage Grove, Oregon

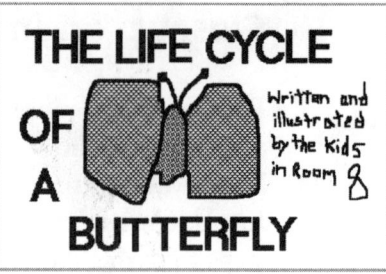
THE LIFE CYCLE OF A BUTTERFLY
Written and illustrated by the kids in Room 8

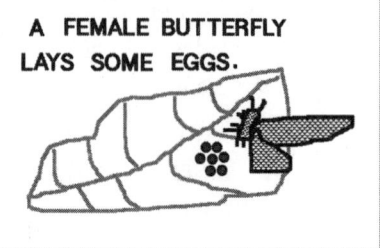
A FEMALE BUTTERFLY LAYS SOME EGGS.

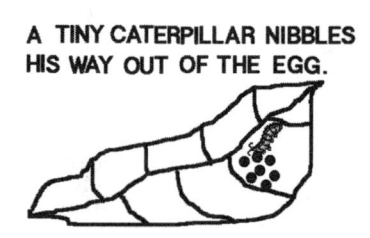
A TINY CATERPILLAR NIBBLES HIS WAY OUT OF THE EGG.

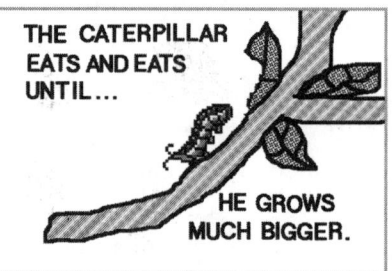
THE CATERPILLAR EATS AND EATS UNTIL... HE GROWS MUCH BIGGER.

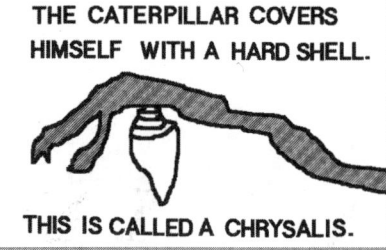
THE CATERPILLAR COVERS HIMSELF WITH A HARD SHELL.
THIS IS CALLED A CHRYSALIS.

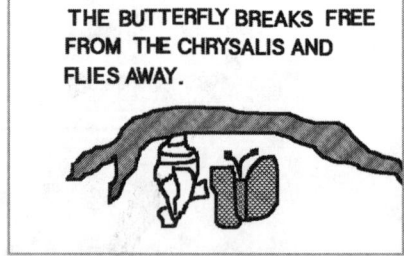
THE BUTTERFLY BREAKS FREE FROM THE CHRYSALIS AND FLIES AWAY.

Who Lives Here?

As part of a unit on habitats, children work in cooperative groups to create Kid Pix presentations about animals, complete with text, pictures, and sound. You can easily adapt the project for any science topic you're teaching.

- As a class, list some of the habitats you've studied. Write these on the chalkboard or on chart paper.

- Divide students into cooperative groups by habitats they want to learn more about. If all students are not equally familiar with Kid Pix, try to form the groups so that each has at least one child who can use the basic Kid Pix tools.

- Have students in each group choose an animal from the selected habitat to research. Guide children in their research by asking them to find, for example, five facts: a description of the animal, a description of its habitat, what it eats, a habit, specialized body parts. Have children organize their information in paragraph or list form. Students in each group can conference with one another to edit and revise their paragraphs.

- Have children in each group work together to create introductions about their habitats.

- Let each group organize research in a Kid Pix slide show presentation, complete with text, pictures, transitions, and sound.

  FOR TEXT: Use the TYPEWRITER tool. Type one fact per slide.

  FOR PICTURES: Choose a pencil or paint tool to create illustrations. Or, scan in pictures created on paper.

  FOR SOUND: Choose RECORD and speak into the computer's microphone. Choose PLAY to listen. If the recording is okay, click SAVE. To record over something, click RECORD again and do it over.

  FOR TRANSITIONS: Complete the slide show by adding transitions between slides. Click on TRANSITION, then preview and select an effect, such as DISSOLVE, WIPE LEFT, WIPE RIGHT, and SHATTER.

- Have groups create title pages to complete the presentations, do a trial run, then share with the class.

Elizabeth Roche
St. Mary's School
Wappingers Falls, New York

Tip

Saving Slide Shows

Save Kid Pix presentations on disk for children to revisit as they wish and share with their families. The STANDALONE option allows you to run the slide show independently of Kid Pix. Or, print individual slides from each presentation and bind to make books to share at home and add to your science library. To print without showing the PLAY SOUND buttons, choose this option under SAVE.

Science

Seasonal Stories

Trees attract children's attention just about any time of the year. In fall, a tree's leaves may be turning colors and dropping. In winter, children may observe tiny buds on bare trees. In spring, new leaves bring life to trees. In summer, leaves on trees provide welcome shade. Learn more about leaves with *I Am a Leaf* by Jean Marzollo (Scholastic, 1999). Then invite children to share their impressions of leaves in each season with this Kid Pix presentation.

- Using the LINE tool, have children divide a page into four parts, one for each season. (You may choose to make a template for children to use.)
- Have children use the TEXT tool or TYPE TEXT option to label the seasons.
- Using the RUBBER STAMP, WACKY PENCIL, and WACKY BRUSH tools, have children create seasonal scenes in each section, showing changes in a tree from one season to the next. (They may use the TREE option in the WACKY BRUSH tool to stamp a tree in each section.) Have them add details to the tree to represent each season. Have them use stamps and other tools to add other seasonal details to each box.
- Invite children who are ready to do more to add captions for each season.

Rhonda Turner
J. O. Schulze Elementary School
Irving, Texas

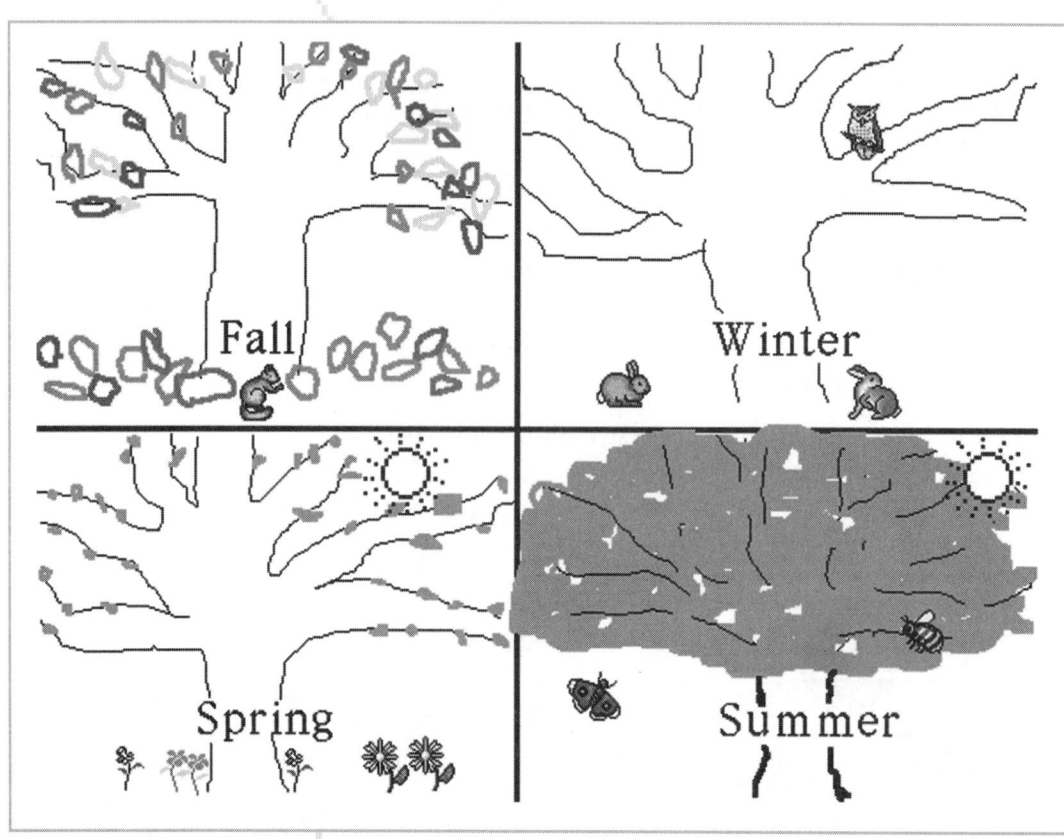

Science

Animals Are Special

In *I Wish I Could Fly* by Ron Maris (Greenwillow, 1987), Turtle wants to fly like Bird, run like Rabbit, dive like Frog, and climb like Squirrel. When it rains, though, and Turtle's shell provides a cozy shelter, he discovers that he has qualities that are just as special. Use this book as a springboard to learning more about what makes animals special.

List the animals from the book on chart paper. Review what makes each animal special. Brainstorm new animals to research. Have children work with a partner to research an animal, finding one special thing that this animal can do. Have students complete the steps that follow to create an illustrated page based on the research. Put pages together, add a cover, and bind.

- Open a new page.
- Use the TEXT tool (largest font) to type the name of the animal on the page.
- Locate the NATURE stamp set from GOODIES and place the stamp of the animal (resized) on the page (or use the WACKY PENCIL to draw a picture).
- Use the TYPE TEXT option to add a sentence about the animal's special characteristic.
- Add your name to the page you create.

Marilee Schuhrke
John V. Leigh School
Norridge, Illinois

Tip

Sharing With a Slide Show

Load students' illustrated pages into the moving vans to make a SLIDESHOW presentation about their animals.

Science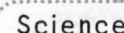

Paper Plate Penguins

Kid Pix makes a terrific science assessment tool. This example shows how children can use the program to demonstrate learning for a unit on penguins. You can adapt the process to almost any science topic: plants, space, baby animals, and so on. Make modifications in the setup to guide children in recording what they know. (For another approach to using Kid Pix for active science assessment, see Life-Cycle Shows, page 56.)

- Have children use the LINE tool to draw a line across a horizontal page, about an inch from the top. Have them draw vertical lines to divide the page into three sections.
- In each section, have children draw and label a stage of a penguin's life—for example, *egg, chick, adult.*
- You may choose to have children write a sentence about each stage, too.
- Have children use paper plates and construction paper to make penguins. Print out pictures and glue to the paper plate section of their penguins.

Karen Alexander
Somerlid Elementary School
Pueblo, Colorado

Science

Pop-Up Science Riddles

Students write clues to go with hidden animals in pop-up pictures. Students will enjoy reading their riddles to one another and showing what pops out of their pictures. You can use the project as an informal assessment tool. You can use the directions that follow to support a lesson on life cycles or eggs. See Variations (below) for other ideas.

- Share *Chickens Aren't the Only Ones* by Ruth Heller (Price, Stern, Sloan; 1993). Let children revisit the story to name animals that hatch from eggs.

- Ask each child to choose an animal that hatches from an egg. Have children find the animal in the Kid Pix stamps, enlarge it by holding down the SHIFT and CONTROL keys, stamp it on the page, and print it. Have children cut out their animal pictures and set them aside.

- Give each child a copy of the egg pattern and strip on page 64. Have children cut out each pattern on the dashed lines and complete the clues on the egg.

- Guide children in folding construction paper in half and placing the egg pattern on the fold as indicated. Have them trace the egg on the construction paper, then cut it out and open it to reveal two eggs (connected at the fold). Ask children to glue the egg pattern with the clues to one side of the construction-paper egg.

- Show children how to fold the strip on the solid lines to make flaps. Help them fold the strip in half, then glue the flaps to the bottom and top of the inside of their egg (close to each side of the egg fold).

- Have children glue their animal picture to the bottom half of the strip so that when they open the egg, the animal pops up.

- Let children share their pop-up riddles with the class. Then place them on display for students to revisit on their own.

Outside egg

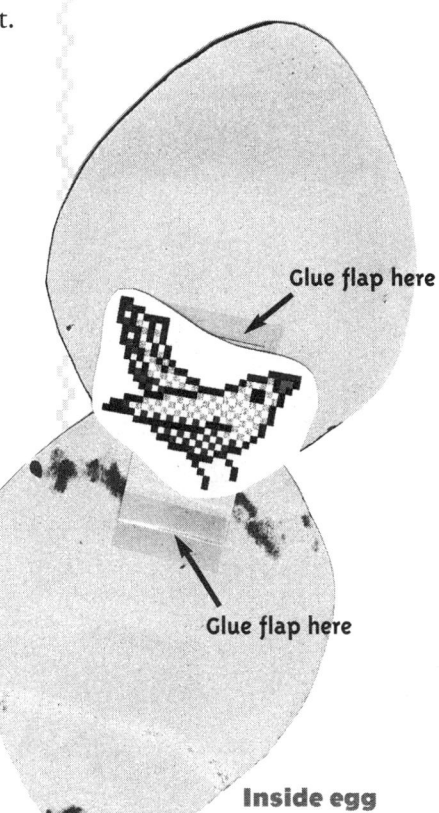

Inside egg

Variations: Read *The Mitten* by Jan Brett (Putnam, 1989) as part of a study of how animals keep warm in winter. Have students make pop-up mittens with pictures of animals inside. Share *Mushroom in the Rain* by Mirra Ginsburg (Macmillan, 1974) for a look at ways animals find shelter in the rain. Have students make mushrooms with animals inside. Explore rain forests with *The Great Kapok Tree* by Lynn Cherry (Harcourt Brace, 1990). Have students make pop-up trees with animals hidden behind the leaves.

Karen Stuart
Westwind Elementary
Wolfforth, Texas

Name _____   Date _____

Slide Show Organizer

Complete one organizer for each slide. Draw your slide in the space below. Include any text that will appear on the slide. Then complete the information at the bottom. Before you write in the slide number, arrange your slides in the order you think is best. When you are sure about the order, write in the number.

Slide Number _____
Font _____ Font Size _____
Transition: _____ Seconds Between Slides
Notes _____
_____
_____

Slide Number _____
Font _____ Font Size _____
Transition: _____ Seconds Between Slides
Notes _____
_____
_____

Slide Number _____
Font _____ Font Size _____
Transition: _____ Seconds Between Slides
Notes _____
_____
_____

Slide Number _____
Font _____ Font Size _____
Transition: _____ Seconds Between Slides
Notes _____
_____
_____

Name _____ Date _____

My Life-Cycle Slide Show

Answer each question. If your answer is Yes, give yourself one point. If your answer is No, leave the space blank.

		Yes	No	Points
1	Do I have a Title and Author page?	☐	☐	_____
2	Do I have a chrysalis picture?	☐	☐	_____
3	Do I have a chrysalis fact?	☐	☐	_____
4	Do I have a larva picture?	☐	☐	_____
5	Do I have a larva fact?	☐	☐	_____
6	Do I have a pupa picture?	☐	☐	_____
7	Do I have a pupa fact?	☐	☐	_____
8	Do I have a butterfly picture?	☐	☐	_____
9	Do I have a butterfly fact?	☐	☐	_____
10	Did I set the Time Slider  for each slide?	☐	☐	_____
11	Did I use Transitions? 	☐	☐	_____

Total Points _____

☀ Write a sentence here that tells what you like most about your slide show.

_____

☀ Write a sentence here that tells something you would do differently in your next slide show.

_____

Pop-Up Riddles

I can _____ .

I have _____ .

I am _____ .

I live _____ .

What am I?

Outside Egg

← Place on Fold →

Strip